Advance P
River of Books: A Life in Reading

"River of Books is a beautiful memoir. Deeply personal, it is moving, dazzling, and spiced with touches of Seaman's slant-wise sense of humor."

—Sara Paretsky,
author of *Pay Dirt* and other V. I. Warshawski novels
and the memoir, *Writing in an Age of Silence*

"River of Books is as exhilarating as a first date, and it delivers: The memoir of a lifelong book lover who brings us her keen, engaging perspective on her own reading and the larger world of books, it will warm you and delight you and make you realize how fabulous reading can be."

—Susan Orlean,
author of *On Animals* and *The Library Book*

"A 'constant reader' who generously advocates for a wide diet of literature, from novels to poetry to narrative nonfiction to essays and all that lie between, Seaman counsels that "the more varied our reading, the more detailed, intricate, and vital our perceptions become."

—Kirkus Reviews

"Donna Seaman reads with her whole body, and *River of Books* is a hymn to her vocation, a testament to her immersions, the story of her transports. The surface is calm, but the water runs deep in this memoir of intense responses, of enchantments and ecstasies."

—Edward Hirsch,
author, *Stranger by Night*,
editor for *100 Poems to Break Your Heart*

River of Books

River of Books

A Life in Reading

Donna Seaman

A collaboration between
the Seminary Co-op Bookstores
and Prickly Paradigm Press
Chicago

© 2024 by Donna Seaman

Published by Ode Books
Prickly Paradigm Press
5751 S. Woodlawn Avenue, Chicago 60637

www.odebooks.com

ISBN: 9781734643565 (paper)
ISBN: 9781958846056 (e-book)

Library of Congress Control Number: 2024946645

Printed in the United States of America on acid-free paper.

For the writers who have inspired and sustained me.

For kindred readers.

For everyone who has nurtured my book passion.

For my loved ones here and now and those gone but forever
with me.

Table of Contents

Never the Same River, Never the Same Book

Just as the river where I step
Is not the same, and is,
So I am as I am not.

—Heraclitus

I have been devoted to reading since the moment marks on a page first came into focus as letters and words. My hunger for reading and my need to dwell on the river of books have propelled and shaped many aspects of my life. Questions arise. Why would a person read so much? What might all that reading mean? In pursuit of answers, I chart the course of my early years in this idiosyncratic and selective reminiscence focused on the place books have held in my life and the places in which I have kept body and soul together by working with books.

I envisioned this as a fairly straightforward narrative, but books steer us in surprising directions and reading leads to more reading and rereading and more questions and lots of meandering. I find myself struck by how much has changed since I learned to read, since I checked out my first library book, since analog gave way to digital. I net books that rise to the surface of my river-of-reading memories, while many more swim below. Ultimately, my hope is to tell just enough of my story to share my love for and reliance on reading, track how reading has propelled my life, and call out books that have been lifeboats, life preservers, anchors, and safe harbors.

Like rivers, books connect places near and far; books and rivers contain and sustain lives. Books can be crystal-clear or murky, serpentine or straight-ahead, shallow or deep, slow-flowing or tumultuous. Rivers and books carry the living and the dead, the past, present, and future. Rivers and books define and transform the terrain across which they flow and the people whose lives depend on them.

Even a metaphorical river has many ports and

portages, tributaries, and coves. I was swept away, spun in whirlpools, hustled by rapids, hurled onto pebbly banks, stuck on sandbars, and snagged in weeds. This look-back has been a retracing and an excavation. An odyssey and a reckoning. This ship's log charts my course through libraries, a bookstore, and the American Library Association, where I joined the staff of *Booklist*, a steadfast book review magazine founded in 1905. Many *Booklist* people end up working there for decades, entranced by the ceaseless, relentless flow of titles and cycle of deadlines. I am one of the perpetually mesmerized, stepping each day into the nurturing, ever-changing, river of books.

The Hudson River, the Source

I believe that we are, at the core, reading animals and that the art of reading, in its broadest sense, defines our species. We come into the world intent on finding narrative in everything: in the landscape, in the skies, in the faces of others, and, of course, in the images and words that our species creates.

—Alberto Manguel

When I was a child I read books. My reading was not indiscriminate. I preferred books that were old and thick and hard. I made vocabulary lists.

—Marilynne Robinson

The book was enormous. The cover shiny and white, festooned with a dragon, a gleaming swirl of scales, claws, fangs, and forked tongue all in fiery purple, gold, and red. I can picture big enticing sans serif letters spelling out *Chinese Fairy Tales*. Or was it *A Treasury of Chinese Fairy Tales*? Or *The Great Big*

Book of Chinese Fairy Tales? Whatever the title, the book was magical. Turning the pages was like opening doors into a palace of long hallways and many chambers and vast windows with panoramic views. The words inside were also large and round and inviting. My mother held the book on our laps as we sat close together, leaning into each other to take in the glory of each page spread. The illustrations were sweeping and expressive. There were people in pointy straw hats, tippy huts, a rippled river, a winding road, rice paddies, oxen, mountains, and clouds. It was while I gazed enraptured at this capacious book that printed words suddenly sharpened into meaning for me. Or so my memory tells me. But this seems to be a fairy tale of my own. I looked for this signal book on the bookshelves in our family home, although that's not where we lived when I was a young child on the cusp of reading, and failed to find it. I searched for it online, assuming that it must have been a readily available volume given that we were a middle-class household of readers, not a clan of rare-book experts. But nothing surfaced to match my vivid recollections.

Until I abruptly became the sole survivor of my loving family and sole owner of our beloved house that, even though I've lived hundreds of miles away for decades, anchored my sense of self.

On the night before what would have been my parents' seventy-third wedding anniversary, in a final act of passionate matrimony, in a departure shocking and mystical enough to feel like the closing scene in an ancient tale of eternal love, my mother and father died unexpectedly, within hours of each other. Their now sadly spellbound house had always been exceptionally neat, welcoming, and bright, vibrant with thoughtfully arranged artworks and lovely objects. It became my task to dismantle this assemblage of tangible evidence of ardently lived lives. I soon discovered that behind this elegantly ordered façade hidden spaces were haphazardly stuffed with fifty years' worth of hastily stashed, random, and forgotten belongings and mementoes redolent with joy, irritation, and sorrow. Here was the physical counterpart to the carefully concealed tumult and pain of two gracious, sociable, and meticulously armored individuals who always made sure to present their most convivial selves to the world.

I found the book of Chinese fairy tales at the bottom of a box beneath other boxes in the basement. The book is large. It's also as battered and worn by love and handling as my favorite old stuffed animal, which I discovered in a rather creepy entombment. I called this humble little dog with the texture and color of oatmeal, bulbous snout, and long floppy ears Morgan and hugged him shapeless. The book, with its peeling cover and loosened spine, is titled simply *Chinese Fairy Tales* with A DELUXE GOLDEN BOOK hovering toward the bottom. The cover image is not of a dragon, but rather of a very pretty, princess-y young woman dressed more in the style of the Italian Renaissance than any Chinese era and her delicate features are Caucasian, perhaps one could say slightly Mediterranean. Basically, she's an aristocratic brunette Barbie. The background window frame and landscape are meant to indicate China, but they look more like a Western stage set than an actual Chinese setting. Dragons do appear drawn in gold on the red endpapers and in a later story, but they are tame compared to the beasts I thought I remembered. The font is Times Roman. My memories are skewed.

I'm surprised by the title page which tells me that these erstwhile Chinese fairy tales were translated by Marie Ponsot, a poet I would read and appreciate decades after my sessions with this dreamy book. Born in New York, Ponsot lived in postwar Paris for a spell and married a French artist. Back in New York, she translated dozens of French children's books into English. These allegedly Chinese fairy tales were filtered through French and English, illustrated by Serge Rizzato, printed in Italy, and published in 1960 in the U.S. with no provenance.

The young woman on the cover of this cultural mishmash is the Princess of Wisteria Wood, which is also the title of the first tale. We're told that Han, an "exceptional" young man, has been pining for a princess to marry in the province of Lu Lung, which is in the grip of a princess shortage. Suddenly "a young slave girl" enters: "'The princess is here and is coming to you.' The girl unrolled a royal carpet from the door to the divan."

What did my mother think, reading this? She was adamant about all people being equal, about human rights and the horrors of racism, antisemitism, and slavery, all of which she talked to me about with arresting intensity when I was very young. In addition to the awkward content, the fairy-tale prose is stilted and dubious. Yet there was so much to enjoy in these clunky hybrid tales, however hijacked. There is mystery, magical beings, infatuation, obstacles, heartbreak, adventure, danger, heroism, and triumph and it all seemed very exciting, especially with Rizzato's elaborate, irresistible illustrations. I wonder if my parents bought this for themselves as well as their little daughters. They loved music (my father would spontaneously pull my mother into his arms to dance around the family room as records spun on the turntable) and musicals, including *The King and I*, a Tony-winning Broadway hit made into a film starring Yul Brynner and Deborah Kerr. My artist mother designed sets for the local community theater when we were little, and *The King and I* was one of her favorite productions. These "Chinese" fairy tales have the same ersatz Asian vibe.

The basement box held another beloved early book, Rudyard Kipling's *Just So Stories* zestfully illustrated by H. B. Vestal. I was tickled by Kipling's clever wordplay in these smart and funny tales of why animals are the way they are. I loved the wiliness of the tricksters and how rhythm and repetition, particularly in "The Sing-Song of Old Man Kangaroo," conveyed motion and emotion. I also adored the quieter humor of the Winnie-the-Pooh books. One favorite poem took the form of a column to embody Winnie-the-Pooh's slow, determined climb up a tree in pursuit of honey. How marvelous it was that words could also form an image. A moody child, I approved of Eeyore. When I was a bit older, I turned to an Old World two-volume set of Grimm's fairy tales; I had the impression they were part of my mother's meager childhood household. The cloth covers are dark and forbidding, while within glow finely etched color illustrations, printed separately and lightly glued to the book's thin pages within embossed frames, punctuating deliciously harrowing tales of otherworldly miseries and impossible tasks in strange places rife with terror and magic.

These off-putting volumes remind me of how I embraced the saying, "Don't judge a book by its cover." I fervently wished that this sentiment pertained to me, too. I did not want to be judged by my cover, my appearance, which I found deplorable. My chronic reading included close and despairing scrutiny of glossy girls' and women's magazines, which I took as scripture for success in conformity. But I never saw any Jewish girls with frizzy curly hair that defied all attempts at smoothing or straightening. And none of the advice or "looks" prescribed seemed potent enough to enable me to achieve the required degree of transformation. How would I ever be popular? Popularity was the ticket to surviving school and it had not been issued to me.

Mocked and harassed, I shriveled inside. Yet I was enthralled by tales of perseverance and guided by the rigors of ballet class, in spite of its own set of humiliations. So, I steeled myself and tried to remain poised and silent, shoulders back, head held high. Mostly I sought refuge in the out-of-body experiences reading provides, grateful to escape the precincts of my odious self. Reading was a compulsion. Antsy at the breakfast table, I read cereal boxes. Stuck in the bathroom, I read labels. Fidgety in class, I concealed novels inside my desk, surreptitiously reading while teachers droned on. Was this all purely about temperament or did being myopic contribute to this predilection?

I didn't know that I couldn't see correctly. The long-soured school nurse knew, but she wasn't telling. Perhaps she felt that she'd done enough by testing my vision, filling out the form, and placing it carefully in my file. I would have lost it anyway, she may have thought, and, besides, it was the parents' responsibility. They should have noticed that their seven-year-old daughter was drifting around in a world as beautifully blurred as an impressionist painting. I found everything wondrous, so detailed up close, so shimmering at a distance. I listened very carefully for keys to what seemed amorphous. I concocted my own assumptions. I was a budding autodidact.

We need to use every tool at hand to help us fully perceive the world and see what others see. Reading is one way to accomplish this, but glasses do help. When I finally received my first pair, I gasped at what they brought into focus. I could hardly walk. I was appalled and overwhelmed. I felt that I'd been cheated, fooled. This was a crisis of being; how could I trust my perceptions, my mind? I faltered as my kind and amused father, whose near-sightedness I'd inherited, guided me out of the optometrist's office. I lifted my foot weirdly high over the threshold and felt faint. The heretofore safe, uniformly gray sidewalk now appeared to be made from a substance riddled with tiny holes. I felt as though I was seeing the cement's molecular structure. I had vertigo. Everywhere I looked new textures leaped out: the speckled and pocked surface of bricks, the veins of surprisingly animated and individuated leaves on trees and bushes, the knobby weave and knit of the clothes of passersby. I was in a new, infinitely more detailed and dimensional world and I was not sure I was up for it. Books have the same impact; they disorient us; they sharpen and correct our perceptions.

***

My reading habit, my trust in literature, and all the illumination that reading bestows determined many of the choices I've made and helped me cope with all that is beyond our control, the vast whirl of epic forces and perpetual chance and change that propel life's infinite complexities and paradoxes. I didn't devote myself to reading because I was instructed to or because it was supposed to be good for us, like vegetables, which I also devour. I read because reading was a way to escape the chaos and the pressure and to make sense of it. Reading was something I could handle, something private, a silent quest. I was engrossed, not overwhelmed. The me I despised disappeared.

Like many book-obsessed kids, I was often told not to read. My habit verged on the antisocial, the hermetic, the transgressive. I was the kind of girl who was told to put down the book and go out and play or join the family or pay attention in class. Reading is protest; it is subversive, a withdrawal, a refusal. Reading is deeply pleasurable. There is a voluptuousness to giving oneself over to language and all that it conjures, an erotic charge in communing with the thoughts and feelings of another. The reader is physically at ease and mentally attentive, gliding away from the actual, the practical, the tedious, the aggravating and into an alternative realm imagined or reported or created in a heady combination of the two. Reading is a form of inebriation, but not of abandon. It's an active state of heightened receptivity. It's transporting. It bestows a sense of accomplishment.

One summer I was a passenger in an old rowboat, enjoying a leisurely turn on a small Wisconsin lake. I found myself looking intently at each pier and house along the shore, and a strangely powerful sensation swept through me: I was reading my surroundings. I was focusing on each detail as though it was a word, each construction a story. The habits of attentiveness and interpretation engendered by reading tunes up one's perception in every circumstance.

What to say to Jamaica Kincaid, whose books I find hypnotic and lacerating? I told her, "I feel as though I read your books with my whole body." Kincaid replied, "I rather like you saying that. I read that way as a writer. I find reading very active. When I was little, we'd recommend books to each other and the highest thing we could say was this book is sweet … we meant it as if it were something you could taste and feel and wear. We loved books."

I was even more struck when Kincaid continued, "And I like that writing is work. I think that I like all the things people say are pleasures to be work because I like working. I like reading because it's working, and I have actually turned reading into a job." Kincaid's comment reverberates. I feel the very same way about my bookish work, my bookish life.

The reader enters the consciousness of another, a realm incandescent with ideas and feelings translated into language as alive as flowers, birds, vines, dolphins. Words are infused with energy like sun dapples on water, embers, rain, surf, wind, bioluminescence. Words are faceted and bright like crystals, shimmering like aurora borealis. As we study the page, we hear the lines, feel the vibration, see the patterns of vowels and consonants and all the images those little symbols magically evoke.

We are also natural-born narrators, continually telling ourselves our stories in our minds, editing and revising as we go. Human nature and life are shaped by this inner commentary. By a continual pulse of language. For those of us fortunate enough to be literate and free to read what we want when we want to, reading is second nature.

Francine Prose writes, "I've always hoped that someone would fund a research project to measure the changes that occur in our brain waves when we lose ourselves in a book. What if it turned out that these changes have a beneficial effect on our health, … What if reading were proved to be even healthier than exercise?" Sedentary as reading is, it is healthful; it is nourishing.

One revelatory evening stays with me. At the time, my entire life seemed to be in jeopardy, and I was clinging to my routine in the hope that going through all the usual motions of my days and nights would protect me. As the sun went down, the wind picked up and the temperature dropped just like they said it would. Other people on the sidewalk hurried along anxiously as the wind shook brittle leaves from bending trees and they skittered across the pavement like small dogs pulling on leashes, their toenails tapping a harassed Morse code. The jittery evening was loud with cryptic messages as awnings and signs shook and creaked in the wind, trash scraped across asphalt, and street and traffic lights trembled in the cold, turbulent air.

The mettlesome wind pulled at my coat and wound my hair around my face as though blindfolding me in preparation for a kidnapping. I turned my head to get free, rounded a corner, and found myself gazing into a long stretch of cafe windows. It was almost an Edward Hopper moment, but instead of detecting loneliness, I read contentment in the body language of the solo diners. Cued by the tilt of one man's head, I saw that he was reading a book that was laid flat on the table before him while he carefully, almost reverently, lifted a spoonful of something hot to his mouth without taking his eyes off the page.

At an adjacent table sat a young woman. Her book was propped against her purse, the edge of her plate keeping the pages open, and she held a toasted bagel frothy with cream cheese before her, waiting to take the next bite as she stared, transfixed, at the print before her. A man was reading the newspaper. He leaned over its folded pages, his hands occupied with a large and unwieldy sandwich; he was graceful and unhurried as he ingested news and nutrients. Eating and reading are such intimate acts, both, I believe, essential to our survival, and I was strangely moved to see them performed so unselfconsciously, in public.

I, too, love to eat and read at the same time. Hungers physical and mental are satisfied in these interludes of rapture and harmony. The body, comfortable yet alert, is fully occupied in nourishing itself, while the mind, rescued from its usual fare of self-nagging and unfulfilled desire, is wholly engaged in assimilating the thoughts of others. In this state of complete absorption, the humblest of foods taste like manna and text acquires a bountiful sensuousness.

I couldn't help but feel that there was an aura of holiness surrounding these eating readers. Nearly every culture known to humankind has evolved rituals that establish and celebrate a connection between language and food. People give thanks before they eat, and many rites and festivities involve the serving and consumption of spiritually significant foods. As poet, essayist, and naturalist Diane Ackerman observes, "If an event is meant to matter emotionally, symbolically, or mystically, food will be close at hand to sanctify and bind it." Words, whether in the form of prayer, song, or even conversation, define the sacredness of food, just as food gives substance to spiritual thought. One blesses the other as the body feeds the mind, the mind feeds the body, and both shelter and nourish the soul.

We say that books provide us with food for thought, and, indeed, reading satisfies our hunger for knowledge and understanding. To break bread beside an open book is to embrace life's sensuousness and spirituality. To live fully and in health, to be free in body, mind, and soul, we need good food and illuminating books and societies that make it possible for all to secure both.

***

Adriance Memorial Library on Market Street in Poughkeepsie, New York, was my first library. In its earliest incarnation it was the state's oldest tax-supported library and the third oldest public library in the country. The Classic Revival structure opened in 1897; it and the books it contained were given to the city by the Adriance family who earned much of their farm-equipment fortune by manufacturing the then innovative Buckeye mower, which sported a floating, double-hinged cutter bar. That was progress then. Now listed on the National Register of Historic Places, Adriance was substantially expanded in the 1920s, then again during the first decade of the twenty-first century.

I experienced bliss in Adriance's dark subterranean children's room, which I remember as a cavern with a ceiling that shimmered as though reflecting an underground pool. It was deliciously cool in the summer, when we spent the most time there, quiet but for the breath and gentle swish of a mysterious life-sustaining element. The books were fishy—shiny, slender, and slippery—gliding off the shelves, schooling and spinning on low tables. My younger sister and I would gather as many as we could in our twiggy little-girl arms, clasping the glinting books to our skinny chests, walking carefully through the shifting light to the pier, the checkout desk, then out into the startling sunshine and the pressing heat. Our old car was a big fish, the heat of its belly making us sweat as the cool books warmed and the vinyl seats nearly scorched our bare legs until we tugged our sandaled feet up to our thighs as the car picked up speed, cutting through the damp air which eddied in through open windows.

This was when words seemed enormous. I remember sitting at my desk in one of my first elementary school classrooms fixated on "island." Everything around me receded and I became an island. I loved how that word was two words but wasn't pronounced that way. I loved the very thought of a small irregularly shaped splotch of land sur- rounded by water. A holdfast, a place of solitude. The "i" of it and the "land." The "is" of it. Another word I marveled over was "march." One of the first poems I remember writing was a walking poem inspired by how march was a noun, a verb, and a month. I could march through chilly puddles in March on the march to school. March was also the name of the family in a book I read over and over again, Louisa May Alcott's *Little Women*.

Whenever I come across an essay or memoir by a woman writer who notes how important *Little Women* was to her, I feel affirmed. One passage that resonates is in *Bone Black*, a deeply moving and bril- liantly structured autobiography of "perceptions and ideas" by bell hooks, a resounding feminist cultural critic. Within this searing account of her experiences as the "problem child" in a tightly run, cash-poor household in a segregated small town in Kentucky, hooks writes about how books helped her survive:

> When I grow up I cannot say what I want to be. I cannot say that I do not want to grow up. I am a child who is sad all the time. They tell us children should be happy, should love to go outside and play. I would rather read books. … I read Laura Ingalls Wilder's *Little House on the Prairie* and Alcott's *Little Women* … I find remnants of myself in Jo, the serious sister, the one who is punished. I am a little less alone in the world.

My fanaticism for *Little Women* was further validated and clarified by Anne Boyd Rioux in her history marking the 150th anniversary of Alcott's novel, *Meg, Jo, Beth, Amy: The Story of Little Women and Why It Still Matters*. Among the many facets of *Little Women*'s long life as an American classic and an evergreen favorite for book-loving girls and women that Rioux investigates is the novel's formative impact on women writers. After discussing its slow rise in the rankings before it was accepted as an important work of literature, a struggle for legitimacy due to its female creator and themes, she observes, "*Little Women* is the book, more than any other, to which American women writers' ambitions can be traced."

Rioux quotes an array of women writers describing what *Little Women* meant to them, including Elizabeth Alexander, Margaret Atwood, Amy Bloom, Maureen Corrigan, Erica Jong, Barbara Kingsolver, Maxine Hong Kingston, Bich Minh Nguyen, Cynthia Ozick, Sara Paretsky, Anna Quindlen, Jane Smiley, Zadie Smith, Gloria Steinem, and Elaine Showalter. Rioux observes, "Ultimately, *Little Women* validated the very idea of a girl developing her own opinions, earning a living, and deciding to become a writer."

It certainly did that for me. Even though I had one sister, not three, and our devoted father was very much present, we, like the March girls, were told to think of others first. My mother basically taught us the Golden Rule, explaining that before we judged anyone else, we should try to imagine what it felt like to be them, to walk a mile in their shoes. This lesson in empathy had a profound impact on me, especially since it's a perspective so readily nurtured by reading.

Jo March was my idol, as she was for so many bookish girls. Jo's scribbling inspired me, but so did her tomboy energy and nerve, her creativity, her lack of vanity and inhibition, her contentment in being alone, pen in hand, and her great love for reading—up in her garret on her "old three-legged sofa," eating apples and turning pages, blissfully elsewhere. She was tall, too, as was I as a girl. I longed for her confidence. Every time I read the novel, I was shocked, bewildered, and awed by her rejection of Laurie's marriage proposal.

***

My second library was housed in a cozy corner in Krieger Elementary School. I was a proud member of the school's Library Club in that handsome brick building bracketed by generous playgrounds and situated at the corner of Grand and Hooker Avenues. I came to appreciate that intersection between the sublime and the profane, dream and reality. What was grand was in the library with its big bay windows. As for Hooker, there was much joking about sex workers on this key artery in our little old river city.

The street was named after James Hooker, a prominent early nineteenth-century businessman who, along with Matthew Vassar, founder of Vassar College, the academic home of a remarkable array of literary stars, was a member of the Improvement Party, a nonpolitical group hoping shore up Poughkeepsie's economy. One ill-fated venture was the launching of two whaling companies, a curious choice, given how far the city is from the ocean. The fledging business got off to a rough start with a mutinous crew who may have murdered their captain and a shipwreck; it sputtered out within a decade. Still, Hooker's name lives on, in spite of one mayor's attempt to change it in 1977. As reported by New York State's oldest newspaper, the *Poughkeepsie Journal*, Mayor Robert E. Ahmed, weary of all the jokes and "bad connotations," proposed renaming the street, but he was thwarted, even mocked. In a sad conclusion to this brief article, staff writer Eric Trilling notes that

"Ahmed also acknowledged he is moving out of his home on Hooker Avenue within 30 days and will be renting a house in the city on Seaman Road. Ahmed said he can't afford his home anymore because of 'financial reversals' over the past two years." This was a difficult time for the city as people of means fled to the suburbs and downtown businesses failed.

We Seamans laughed about Seaman Road, a lovely curving street with handsome old houses and tall trees, a byway to which we, of Russian Jewish and Polish Jewish descent stamped with an Ellis Island-improvised, anglicized, seafaring last name, had zero connections. It ran through what was once Cedarcliff, the sweeping estate of John Ferris Seaman (1844–1915); there is also a Ferris Lane. In 1924, those Seamans donated their land to the YWCA, which built a facility with one of the first indoor swimming pools in Dutchess County. Nearby was the tennis club which was still closed to Jews when I was a child.

The name Seaman, a neat, English, fresh-off-the-boat solution to what would have been viewed as an unpronounceable foreign name, sparked my lifelong love of dictionaries. Initially I liked my last name's call-out of the ocean, of the sea. But why did spring-loaded little boys snort and giggle? Mortified and mystified, I wrote down a list of possible alternative spellings, hauled open our Webster's, and discovered that knowledge can be slimy and empowering. For my Manhattanite grandfather, this punning New World name seemed to be destiny when a friend encouraged him to enlist in the navy to avoid being drafted for trench combat in World War I. Seaman Seaman was trained as a cook. He later performed in vaudeville, sold insurance, and went fishing whenever he could slip away. His son and his family were among the alien riffraff who descended on Poughkeepsie, ninety miles north of New York City, at the beckoning of IBM. This small historic Hudson Valley city was all too-often closed-minded and prejudiced as brash, future-propelling IBM boomed, buying up land; building sprawling, state-of-the-art manufacturing facilities and office buildings surrounded by acres of parking lots; and bringing in battalions of outsiders. I detected the resentment against us as a girl but didn't understand it until much later.

I hadn't seen this particular locale for social friction explored in fiction until I read Toni Morrison's only known short story, "Recitatif," first published in an anthology in 1983 and which I first read in book-champion Glory Edim's *On Girlhood: 15 Stories from the Well-Read Black Girl Library*. "Recitatif" was subsequently published on its own with an enlightening introduction by Zadie Smith. The story begins when two abandoned eight-year-old girls, Twyla and Roberta, find themselves sharing a room in a shelter. We know that one is white and one is Black, but as Morrison sets out their differences—one is grateful for the food, the other hates it; one's mother is ill, the other mother "dances all night"—we are left trying to guess their racial identities while simultaneously realizing how thoroughly programmed we are to think in that mode, which makes us wonder why it's so important. As the story strides forward in time, class emerges as another divide as Twyla and Roberta reconnect as wives and mothers in Newburgh, New York, a boom-and-bust Hudson River town undergoing IBM-generated gentrification where people take to the streets in vehement protest against or for school busing.

***

The Library Club confirmed my preference for quiet spaces alive with the clamor of books, for physical order and inner wildness. All those upright spines contained storms and conflicts, love and pain. The library was an arsenal and a pantry, a pharmacy and a temple. I loved that sunny room of honey-varnished wooden shelves, big solid tables, and high-backed chairs. I loved shelving books and neatening slippery stacks of magazines stacked in reverse chronological order. I liked the rubber date stamp which we struggled to advance with a straightened paper clip so as not to get ink all over our hands and put books at risk. I purred over the lined cards in the cardboard pockets pasted inside the books. The flapping due-date sheets. The little wooden boxes in which we filed the cards. I admired the librarian, Mrs. Madison, who was kind and demanding, dishy and proper. I read my way through that little school library, industriously consuming a series of kids' biographies and armloads of fiction. Library posters featured a cartoonish bookworm, and it was considered cute to use that term to describe a reader like me, but I loathed the name. Insecure as I was, at least I wasn't a spineless, wriggling creature, nor a creepy insect that destroyed books.

Exhilarated in the library, I was bored and impatient in the classroom, always doodling, watching the slow second hand on the big wall clock, looking out the window, and daydreaming. I disliked being a child, annoyed at the condescension with which adults addressed us and keenly aware that most of what we were told were lies or mere shards of the truth dispensed to keep us in line. I bristled. I seethed. I read *National Geographic* and *Life* magazine cover to cover as an antidote to the dopey *Weekly Reader*. I embraced the flinty word "cynic" with dark recognition. I felt electrocuted when I learned about the atomic bomb.

My young brain could not make sense out of a weapon that could end life on earth. I short-circuited with fear and anger as I gazed at photographs of mushroom clouds and read about fallout, nuclear winter, Hiroshima and Nagasaki. We had air raid drills at school that were clearly preposterous, mere ritual. Nothing we did in our classrooms or hallways would keep us safe.

My nuclear fear and vexation eventually steered me to works of reportage and history, including the seminal *Hiroshima*, by John Hersey, and *The Fate of the Earth*, by Jonathan Schell. I've also been struck by imaginative fiction that embeds the nuclear paradox in characters' psyches and lives: novels that dramatize the cosmic ludicrousness and terror of our reliance on what seems like a plot device in a dark satire, the very real, precarious, and chillingly well-named MAD doctrine, mutually assured destruction. The fingers-crossed spell that has held the world's nuclear powers in check.

Leslie Marmon Silko grew up on the Laguna Pueblo Reservation in New Mexico, atomic ground zero, and her poetic and haunting first novel, *Ceremony*, explores the insidious impact of the confluence of racism, genocide, war, radiation, and the bomb. Don DeLillo taps into the haunting forces unleashed by the inception of the nuclear age in the many-voiced *Underworld*. Its cast includes Nick Shay, a waste-management expert burdened by a violent past who contemplates the handling of plutonium: "Waste is a religious thing. We entomb contaminated waste with a sense of reverence and dread." And artist Klara Sax, who has created a monumental work in the middle of the bomb-test-scoured desert out of decommissioned B-52s, bombers that once carried (and did not release) nuclear bombs. In Lydia Millet's trippy and revelatory time-travel tale, *Oh Pure and Radiant Heart*, a Santa Fe librarian and her gardener-husband end up giving sanctuary to three legendry atomic physicists—chain-smoking Robert Oppenheimer, depressed Enrico Fermi, and irrepressible Leo Szilard—three geniuses who are utterly bewildered to find themselves in the twenty-first century.

Exasperated by my indignation and gloominess, my chic, socially conscious, activist and artist mother called me an "old woman" when I was all of seven years old. At least in the library, surrounded by books and magazines, free to browse the shelves and think about what to read next, I felt hopeful and inspired instead of belittled and oppressed. I still have my Library Club pin.

Some of the old books in our house were acquired "antiquing," a favorite form of weekend car adventures in the curvaceous and secretive Hudson Valley where small farms and large estates are nestled among stony hills. My father, an electrical engineer by trade and a photographer for fun (he set up a darkroom in our basement), and my artist mother, both raised in the Bronx, loved the narrow, winding roads in what my city cousins called the "sticks." We four would cruise around, looking for barns turned into antique shops, especially in late summer and on bright and tangy autumn days, emerging from the car on percussive gravel or carpets of golden pine needles or flame-colored leaves or flattened, brown grass, stretching car-cramped legs and dawdling a bit in the fresh air before heading in to examine objects of iron and porcelain, cloth and brass, wood and ivory jumbled on old tables, many loosely constructed out of boards, doors, and sawhorses. Maybe one such hunt netted the set of Charles Dickens novels with the dark brown covers, gold embossed letters, and thin pages dense with small print.

What induced me to take *David Copperfield* down from the shelf one summer? Elated at the prospect of a child-free vacation, my in-love parents dropped their two coltish daughters off at an old-fashioned boarding house in Stanford, New York, where my mother's mother and her second husband, my mother's stepfather, had been summering for decades. A big old frame house run by a Mrs. Green, it featured oval hooked rugs on shiny wood floors and a big front porch ranked with wooden rocking chairs bright with tie-on cushions. The porch faced the two-lane highway and my little sister and I would sit and rock energetically, stretching our arms way up to wave to passing truckers who waved back and blew their horns.

Inside was a nineteenth-century time capsule, with a fine old grandfather clock ticking and chiming; carefully maintained furniture with floral-patterned upholstery, period paintings and sketches on wall-papered walls, and a decent old piano that my grandmother played in the evenings. My sister and I shared a bedroom upstairs with brass beds covered with quilts and lace-curtained windows looking out on the vast yard and kitchen garden and a little sink with ancient fittings and a drain stopper on a chain. A large flowery pitcher sat in a matching basin on a small shelf nearby, harking back to the boarding house's pre-indoor-plumbing days. I brought *David Copperfield* along, beginning my long habit of packing books first, then fitting clothes around them, and young David became my secret imaginary playmate. We also pestered the kind and friendly college-age staff for jars to catch grasshoppers and lightning bugs and for company more intriguing than the oldsters who embarrassed us with their doting adoration and annoyed us with their do's and don'ts.

Here I experienced the delectable simultaneity of dueling existences that reading provides. There was all the excitement of being away from our parents and our normal routine and plunged into this little snow-globe world of elders and antiques where we were pampered little guests in a house built around the time Dickens was serializing his semiautobiographical tale of a man looking back at his up-and-down childhood. I fell in book-love with young David as I read that multilayered novel of boyhood, fractured family, class, gender expectations, law, and so much more to the best of my absurdly limited abilities and frame of reference. I remember all this vividly, but I wasn't able to pinpoint my age, though my fascination with the lively and attractive young woman and man helping run the place made me think I was on the verge of adolescence.

As I sorted through the stashes of papers and photographs squirreled away in our family home, I came across a crumbling box of memories my father shoved into the attic crawl space. I was stunned by what he kept. Here was a fifth-grade report card

from one of my favorite teachers, the creative, magnetic, stylish, and worldly Sonia Brousalian, whom
I've always been grateful to for demonstrating that
reading and the arts are intimately interconnected,
mutually nurturing, and equally significant. She
wrote in her strong, forward-leaning script, "Donna
is a sensitive, intelligent person. She lacks some confidence in herself. When this is overcome, she should
do very well. I find her to be quite helpful in class."
"Person" she writes. Not "student," not "child," not
"girl," but a person in her own right.

Though on target, "lacks some confidence"
was vastly understated. I was a festering wound of
self-hatred. How was I helpful in class? By being
attentive and enthralled? I received top marks for
"Behavior" and "Work Habits," but not for "Prepares
work neatly" (my handwriting remains atrocious).
High marks were awarded for "Reading," too, even
though one of the subcategories is "Understands
what he reads." What I remember best about that
year, along with Ms. Brousalian's vivacious bril-
liance, was a rare sense of belonging and a deepened

commitment to reading. The latter helps explain a more startling discovery in my father's archive: cheerful book reports written during the summer after that good school year ended, including one for *David Copperfield*, composed a month or so after I turned twelve. Evidence suggests that since I insisted on spending so much of my time reading, my father tied receiving my pittance of an allowance to writing about the books that captivated me. Smart, witty, and circumspect, he helped set my life's path.

My report makes it clear that I did, indeed, read all of Dickens' novel and reveled in the many vivid characters. I list a slew of them (those indelible names!), then write, "The book is so good and seems so real I remember 12 other characters plus dozens and dozens of people that were less important in the main plot of the story." I continue with, "It is hard to briefly describe *David Copperfield*," a phrase that expresses my feeling to this day as I finish a novel of profound depth and complexity and despair of being able to review it succinctly as I'm required to do professionally. I continue, "The book had a little of everything in it. Parts of it were extremely sad or happy. It even got very adventurous and suspenseful." Then I efficiently summarize the plot. I do not confess to my infatuation with the young hero.

I hadn't looked at *David Copperfield* in years. Nor had I been inside a library during the terrifying first year-and-a-half of the COVID-19 pandemic; my library card had even expired. So, one blustery Sunday in November, a day draped in low-hanging bunting clouds of purpling gray and bruised blue, I walked over to what I will likely always think of as the "new" Independence branch. For years our Northwest Side neighborhood had one of the city's last funky old storefront libraries. With library commissioner Mary Dempsey at the helm from 1994 to 2012, Chicago built 44 new branches in as many neighborhoods. Dempsey later said, "I've purchased and knocked down more liquor stores, more no-tell motels, more really crummy and dilapidated, burned-out buildings in neighborhood after neighborhood and replaced them with libraries than I'd ever thought

I'd do in my life."

In our languishing old branch, the floors creaked beneath worn, discolored carpeting; the thickly varnished wood chairs were heavy and hard to move. The neatly patterned pressed-tin ceiling was blurred by successive coats of paint; the fluorescent lights of vaguely pinkish and yellowish hues flickered and faintly hummed. It housed a small, humble, much-handled collection, but I often found what I sought or came across felicitous surprises. I enjoyed seeing kids at the small tables, adults on various missions. Some were seeking shelter, others a safe place to read the paper for free; some just needed to get out of the house, others were fleeing loneliness in a place of sharing where a nod from a stranger or a quiet conversation affirmed one's existence. And like every library, no matter its size or finances, this one pulsed with the murmuring voices pressed between book covers.

I love that neighborhood libraries are called branches. Branch suggests the life force that courses through books, and it makes me think of the tree of knowledge, tree houses, and pages as leaves. I was thrilled to find this expressed so vividly by Edward Hirsch in his poem, "Branch Library." He writes, "I wish I could find that skinny, long-beaked boy / who perched in the branches of the old branch library." Hirsch's wistful memories of his young self as a "birdy boy" finding sustenance in books stirs me, mirroring, as it does, my bookish young self.

The Chicago Public Library rose from the ashes of the Great Chicago Fire and, in a bit of magic realism, made its first home in an enormous water tank that survived the conflagration, a circular structure at the southeast corner of LaSalle and Adam streets. The first librarian, in keeping with this watery legacy, was William Frederick Poole. Great Britain sent the decimated yet quickly reviving city a generous gift of 8,000 books to establish a free library (as opposed to private libraries requiring membership fees). Delivered with a proclamation of sympathy from Queen Victoria, this bounty inspired the passing of the Illinois Library Act of 1872, which, to quote the Chicago Public Library's website, "authorized cities to establish tax-supported libraries throughout the state."

One-hundred-and-fifty-years later, our neighbor-hood branch is one of three partnering with the Chicago Housing Authority, signifying the link between home and library that so many readers feel. This bright new branch occupies the lower floors of a white building with bright colors framing the windows of the apartments above. The image of a large owl is worked into the façade facing one of Chicago's immense six-corner intersections where a diagonal street lances the grid. An emblem of wisdom, knowledge, and intelligence, the owl is the library system's totem animal. The Harold Washington Library (named in honor of Chicago's first Black mayor who was passionate about reading and who died at the start of his second term in 1987) has five enormous aluminium owls perched on the roof at each corner and over the main entrance.

Our little library looks like it might be constructed out of LEGOs, sitting neat and happy on a busy street in a neighborhood that has stubbornly repelled gentrification. The owl presides over a liquor store, empty or unidentified storefronts, auto mechanic

shops, rundown apartment buildings, and a scatter-
ing of modest family restaurants serving Mexican,
Thai, and Middle Eastern cuisines. As I enter the
glass-fronted Independence branch, I see a small boy
near the check-out counter struggling to hold on to
two large, slippery picture books. The ground floor
is outfitted with low stacks and cozy areas for young
readers. A nearly room-filling staircase occupies most
of the open space, providing Parthenon-like seating
for readers or audiences, the white steps punctuated
by square cushions in the same bright colors as those
surrounding the building's windows. The teen and
adult books are upstairs in a loft area with glass walls
looking onto a wooden deck fringed with prairie
grass. I take a deep breath behind my mask, happy
to be among books. Upstairs I first notice a librarian at a desk, intent on a computer screen, then a
young man looking at the "new nonfiction" shelves.
A large man is seated at a reading table at a strange
angle. He's wearing many layers of clothing, his face
wrapped in a grimy scarf. He could be a character
out of the Dickens novel I was there to check out. He

slept undisturbed. At another nearby table a public computer monitor sports a post-it note stating "Out of Order."

There is a tendency to romanticize libraries, and I do lean that way even though I'm fully aware of the hard facts pertaining to these public spaces. Bette Howland, a long-overlooked, then ardently reclaimed Chicago writer of live-wire incisiveness and shredding wit ("She was giving him a hard time; people give what they can.") knew firsthand that while public libraries are sanctuaries they are also places of conflicts and confrontations, desperation and bizarreness, a pooling place of woes and the woebegone. Though her work had the support of Saul Bellow during his long tenure at the University of Chicago and earned her Guggenheim and MacArthur fellowships, Howland had a tough life.

After a debacle at the University of Iowa Writers' Workshop over the formatting of her thesis, she worked part-time for a spell at the Chicago Public Library's Uptown branch, starting in 1968. A compassionate, trenchant, and hilarious ethnographer of

eccentricities and dysfunction, Howland wrote about
the library in the story "Public Facilities":

> But the one outstanding fact of life at Borglum
> Branch—the fact that so many of our patrons
> seemed to have nowhere else of any signifi-
> cance to go—was never mentioned. It was
> unmentionable ... Regulars didn't even have
> library cards. What for? Who needed a card?
> They practically lived in the library.
>
> The most popular volume in the branch
> library was the medical dictionary. You had to
> ask. It was kept under lock and key in a glass
> case. Customers coughed behind their hands,
> trying not to look worried about their health.
> As if their troubles weren't obvious enough.

Fortunate to have always had a home, for me libraries
have been oases, treasure houses, places of discovery
and employment. One goes hunting and gathering
in a library, not shopping. You don't have to worry
about what you can afford, only about what you can
carry. No money will change hands, yet goods will
be acquired. And while the physical item will be
returned, your internalization of each book is yours
as long as memory serves. One stalks the stacks with

a reverence not unlike that felt in a museum, but here you can touch and sample and take. On this chilly day, I took home a copy of *David Copperfield*, a paperback edition that showed no evidence of ever having been read. As I began reading it, I marveled at the perseverance, comprehension, and delight of my younger self, at my summer-long infatuation with Dickens' hero. Falling in love is often part of the reading matrix. Marilynne Robinson writes, "I think fiction may be, whatever else, an exercise in the capacity for imagined love, or sympathy, or identification."

We readers do fall in love with characters or feel in sync with them or appalled by them. But as I fled childhood, it was writers I came to adore, the creators of these word-beings who arouse such strong emotions. What an endlessly strange and marvelous feat it is to so convincingly imagine a richly dimensional human being navigating complicated predicaments in a convincingly rendered world.

***

Childhood is marked by rites of passage formal and improvised. Mine were of the latter. One was the swimming test one had to pass to be allowed in the deep water of the man-made lake at the Jewish Community Center's country outpost. We spent long, happy days there, frolicking in the kids' area delineated by ropes held up with colorful buoys. A bowl-shaped lake with a sandy bottom, it was a wet playground, and we stayed in the water until our fingers pruned. But every child had eyes on the center of the lake where a large, anchored raft was inhabited by a flock of rowdy teens. To reach that promised square, one had to prove that one could swim and stay afloat. A lifeguard with a whistle, stopwatch, and clipboard accompanied hopeful adolescent swimmers in a small rowboat. We had to perform various strokes and tread water. It felt like a baptism or bat mitzvah. It was both a submergence and an ascent.

I also sought the deeper waters at the public library, asking to enter the upstairs stacks, where the real books lived. The thick, solid, somber books vibrating with secrets that illuminated the mysteries of the adult world. Here would be liberation from the withholding and evasiveness I chafed under as a child. Here were portals to the past, to other places, other lives, and other minds, the most puzzling of realms. I felt so locked into my own worries and fears, so clutched up with the tedium of self-consciousness, of frustration with my shortcomings and flaws. I longed for enthralling, provocative, transporting stories. I was gently informed by the librarian, however, that I had to have my parents' permission before I could check out the big books.

I was disappointed but not surprised and not too worried. After all, my parents were readers. As poor kids in the Bronx, they headed to the library after school and on weekends, happier in that place of possibilities than in their unhappy homes. In those hulking buildings each apartment was configured the same way behind identical doors that lined the halls like spaced books on shelves, while behind each door unscrolled a unique story. My parents were determined to create very different lives for their children in the new little split-level house they bought, tending to the little yard, adding a back patio, and planting young trees, rosebushes, and forsythia. This was their storybook house, and they were going to have a whole and wholesome family unlike the fractured households they escaped as soon as they could, marrying young.

But not even their love and zeal for cleanliness and order kept the world at bay, and their daughters were not rosy storybook characters. We were high-strung, thorny, and porous. We had antennae for tragedy and injustice. I did read for comfort, hypnosis, and fun, devouring Nancy Drew, Sherlock Holmes, Agatha Christie, and Archie comics. But I was equally avid for serious books. Books that stunned and rocked me. Books I couldn't fully comprehend but which illuminated some aspects of the enigmatic adult world. I kept lists of books I wanted to read and lists of the books I finished with comments and questions. I kept lists of words new to me and their definitions. Eventually, as my reading missions became more focused, I began to notice which publishers published books I loved most and I kept a list of those, too, cued by their neatly evocative logos: the Knopf borzoi in full stretch, the W. W. Norton seagull in flight, Simon & Schuster's sower.

When I was ten, my parents gave me a little locked diary. The red leather cover was embossed with gold: "My Diary." The lined pages were edged in gold, and the little lock and key were also gold. I sort of liked this fussiness, though I knew that nothing I would write would merit it. Yet that didn't stop me from filling its pages, and many more notebooks of more utilitarian design thereafter, none in need of locks because my in-haste handwriting is damn-near indecipherable. To compound that, as an elusive, nearly feral teen, I wrote in tiny print in faint pencil, the visual equivalent of whispering. No one would have the patience or interest to tackle that. I also refused to use capital letters.

Somehow the practice of capitalizing proper nouns and even the first words in sentences started to seem morally dubious to me. I was especially affronted by "I." Why was this singular pronoun capitalized and other pronouns are not? Isn't the elevation of "I" the source of so many problems? Where this pseudo-radical stance came from, I do not recall. Did it stem from my reading poems by E. E. Cummings (also known as e e cummings)? Or did I revel in Cummings's poems because of my aversion to capital letters? Whatever the cause-and-effect, I was inspired by the way poetry in general used punctuation more freely than standard prose—Dickinson's dashes—and I was thrilled by Cummings' word play, his combining and splitting of words, inventing words, embedding parenthetical observations in odd spots, making you feel that he was confiding in you. "Mud-luscious" and "puddle-wonderful" felt so right and somehow sexy to me. I also sensed the darker dimension in Cummings, the chill in the shadows even on a sunny day.

***

We speak of many things when we speak of coming of age, but for me it was catalyzed by reading about human violence against ourselves and other species. When I first learned the most basic facts about slavery in America and the genocidal conquest of Native

Americans some part of me cracked and broke. The damage increased exponentially the more I read about the Holocaust, the atomic bomb, and the slaughter of buffalo and passenger pigeons and whales—the industrial assault against nature. I felt stained and scoured by the past and feared that the future had already been poisoned, chained, and stolen. I was mutely furious and deeply distrustful.

An eighth-grade social studies assignment required students to speak to the class. My presentation was about the Trail of Tears, a chapter in American history that so staggered and outraged me, I wrote a rant and somehow overcame my acute stage fright to storm my way through it even as I began to cry. I sat down shaken, in a fog of embarrassment and agony. Any remaining tatters of childhood innocence burned away in my rage. This is what Holden Caulfield grapples with—I read *The Catcher in the Rye* over and over again, along with J. D. Salinger's piercing stories. But I had never come across a close rendering of my classroom meltdown until I read Jay Cantor's epic of 1960s radicalism, the novel *Great Neck*.

The opening section brings us into a sixth-grade class in this prosperous Long Island suburb, which seems like the Promised Land to its Jewish denizens, some of whom are Holocaust survivors, including the sixth-grade teacher who has his students give oral reports on various countries in Europe. Hypersensitive misfit and future brilliant comic-book artist Billy Green is assigned France just as his father brings home "an encyclopedia of Jewish history." Now, gasping and sobbing, he shares what he has learned about Jews in France under the Nazis. As Billy struggles to recount the increasing atrocities, Cantor illuminates the thoughts of Billy's only sort-of friend, Arthur Kaplan, one of several classmates who will become radicalized during the civil rights and antiwar movements, and their teacher, who is harboring deep traumas having barely survived the Drancy internment camp outside Paris.

> Billy took a Pez dispenser from the pocket of his windbreaker and jabbed himself repeatedly in the cheek with the joker-face cap. "And Jews weren't allowed in swimming pools." (*jab*) "And Jews couldn't go to the

Squire, or the Playhouse." (*jab*) "And Jews couldn't eat in restaurants." (*jab*) "And Jews couldn't go to the library." (*jab*) "And Jews had to ride in the last car on the train." (*jab*) "And they could tell who was a Jew by his yellow star and if someone thought you were a Jew because you had a big nose like my father does, and you weren't wearing your star, he could call the police and the policeman would arrest you because you weren't wearing your star and put you in the prison camp. And Jews," Billy said, weeping again. "And Jews." He paused. "Jews," he said quietly. And "Jews," he whispered. "Jews. Jews." Then he stopped, and just stared at them while he rhythmically smashed the peaked cap of the dispenser's green joker head in and out of his flesh, raising a red sore on his cheek...

What I Hope for in Books

Arresting voices.

Exacting descriptions.

The unexpected.

The confluence of inner and outer worlds.

Interconnections intimate and cosmic.

Nature illuminated on scales minute and monumental.

Emotions exactingly conveyed.

New perspectives.

Old stories retold with fresh insights.

Startlingly stories that illuminate the stamp of the past
on the present, the present on the future.

The pursuit of social justice.

The wonders of science.

History true and holistic.

The big picture.

A microcosm.

Metaphors and similes of startling inventiveness and aptness.

The fusion of the actual and the made-up.

Crisp, succinct sentences.

Long, riverine, meandering, nuanced, disconcerting, funny, gorgeous, lyrical, elevating, burrowing, spiraling, complex, erotic, shimmering, percussive, many-faceted, suspenseful, unnerving, dizzying, breathtaking sentences.

Words as smooth from use as pebbles on the beach.

Words as piercing as thorns.

Unfamiliar words that send you to the dictionary.

Love.

Doubt.

Wit.

Spiritual questioning.

Irreverence.

Awe.

Philosophical debates.

Satire.

The nexus of body and mind.

The extension of possibility.

Suspense.

Irony.

Empathy.

Complexity.

Perplexity.

Hilarity.

Elucidation.

Resonance.

Musicality.

Artistry.

Food for thought.

Soul food.

Reading High

But words empower us, move us beyond our
suffering, and set us free. This is the sorcery
of literature. We are healed by our stories.

—Terry Tempest Williams

Billy Green, Jay Cantor's devastated child of conscience in *Great Neck*, deploys a PEZ dispenser, a
cartoony plastic object designed to sell pepper-
mint candy to children, as a scourge that allows
him to respond to anguish with physical pain.
Manufactured in Austria, a location tied to the
abominable history Billy confronts, PEZ was first
marketed to adults as a breath mint in dispensers
resembling a cigarette lighter. In 1955, a few years
after the mints arrived in the U.S., the company
decided to reel in children with cartoon icons
Mickey Mouse, Popeye, and Donald Duck, topping

PEZ dispensers with their colorful heads. They took characters from the ever-burgeoning Disney catalog, various movie franchises, and DC Comics, the original home for Billy's totem figure, the Joker, Batman's diabolical archenemy and a psychopathic supervillain. The Joker PEZ head is clown-creepy with its enormous, red-lipped smile outlining car-grill teeth beneath a sharp nose, jutting cheekbones, drilling green eyes, and malevolently arched eyebrows. Cheap, mass-produced, unnerving: it's the perfect plastic embodiment of the mad genocidal violence that leaves Billy unhinged.

I knew only the most fundamental facts about the Holocaust when I read *The Diary of Anne Frank* for the first time in a trance of wonder and guilt, horror and sorrow as I neared the end of my safe Jewish American childhood. I had a vague sense of the restrictions and fears the Frank family and other Jews faced in Nazi-occupied Amsterdam as they were forced to accentuate their vulnerability by wearing the yellow star, but I was mostly caught up in Anne Frank's microcosm of relationships and longing as she recorded her family's dangerous existence hidden in what they called the Secret Annex.

Their holdfast was concealed behind the offices and warehouse of Otto Frank's spice company in a tall, narrow, eighteenth-century canal row house. As a girl, I was amused and touched by Anne's decision to address her diary entries to "Dearest Kitty," but it's freshly affecting to reread her reasoning for this as she muses over her lack of "one true friend" and explains: "To enhance the image of this long-awaited friend in my imagination, I don't want to jot down the facts in this diary the way most people do, but I want the diary to be my friend, and I'm going to call this friend *Kitty*."

As a girl just a bit younger than Anne Frank when the book begins, I was humbled by her maturity, eloquence, and insights as she creates this indelible testament to terror, isolation, fortitude, creativity, and hard work. I didn't realize then what is now recognized, that Frank was a serious writer who thoughtfully revised her work. She was thirteen when she began writing, fifteen when she began

editing and rewriting earlier entries as she continued to record fresh episodes chronicling life in the
Secret Annex. This careful refinement was inspired
by a radio broadcast in which a Dutch lawmaker in
exile in London called for eyewitness accounts of
the German occupation and the suffering it caused.
Frank ardently embraced this summons to document
the truth of the situation, her life, and her thoughts,
a mission, she felt, that infused her efforts, her very
existence, with meaning and purpose.

Frank's hellish world, her courage, conviction,
and artistry, put me to shame for my petty laments
and I embraced this perspective. I was reading hun-
grily to learn more of the world. Each book expanded
my mind-map of the human condition, of Earth and
the cosmos, and as grim as much of that knowledge
was, on good days it felt subtly empowering.

Another book in my early rereading rotation
was a young-adult novel about a twelve-year-old girl
who became one of the first of two Black students
to attend a previously all-white public junior high
school in the South. I liked to imagine I would have

befriended and defended them against the nasty stupid little racists and the terrifying parents who injected their children with hate. I remember being captivated and outraged by this book, but while I could summon up a hazy memory of its cover, I could not pull up the title or author from the deep well of reading past. But when I searched for the book online, it surfaced instantly. It turns out that I am far from alone in my admiration for *Mary Jane* by Dorothy Sterling. First published in 1959, five years after the landmark Supreme Court decision *Brown v. Board of Education of Topeka*, Sterling's groundbreaking novel went through numerous printings into the 1970s and was translated and published around the world.

As I reread *Mary Jane* many years later in another century, I was charmed and affected all over again. Sterling is a clear-minded storyteller on a mission skilled in dodging the pitfalls of "message" fiction. She has Mary Jane, a beloved child in a loving, accomplished family, tell her story, so that readers experience her perception of the barrage of frenzied hate she and Fred face as they walk—"Heads up. Eyes front."—through a screaming mob of white adults and children to reach the front door of the school. They also endure shoving, slurs, and other forms of hate-driven aggression, hostility, and condescension in hallways, classrooms, and the cafeteria. Because Fred is athletic, his situation eases a bit, but Mary Jane remains isolated, turning to books for company as she sits alone at lunch. Eventually a mutual love for animals sparks a friendship between Mary Jane and Sally, a girl so pale she often turns crimson. When they are spotted sitting together at lunch and walking and talking together outdoors, white people call Sally's parents in indignation and disgust.

Born in New York City in 1913, Dorothy Dannenberg Sterling was raised in a secular household in which they celebrated Santa-Claus Christmases and Easter-Bunny Easters, as did we. In her memoir, *Close to My Heart,* Sterling wrote, "I did not hear the word 'Jew' until I was five or six and our family and Uncle Manny's were having a picnic in the country. We were sitting under a tree eating sandwiches and drinking lemonade from paper cups when some farm children drew near and shouted, 'Dirty Jews! Dirty Jews! Kikes!'" Eventually, Sterling, who lived to be 95, would face discrimination as a Jew, a woman, a feminist, a communist, and an antiracist writer.

We were not a religious family, but we were proudly Jewish, and I was taught to respect and cherish our heritage. My mother, a born feminist, rejected the gender inequality embedded in traditional Judaism. My father agreed to a bar mitzvah to please his father, whom he adored, but he otherwise rejected religion in favor of morality, reason, and science. My free-thinking, upright, compassionate parents distilled Jewish teachings down to an essential form of humanism based on the call to treat others as you want to be treated, yes, as mentioned, the reverberating Golden Rule. Their parental commandments were to value truth and responsibility. To recognize that you are part of a family and a community and to not put yourself first. To know that what you think, what you do, and how you live matter. We were taught to respect others, which ranged from simple courtesy to recognizing that everyone is equal, that everyone has their hardships and joys. And to do our best to do the right thing even when doing so is difficult or painful. Especially then.

My mother talked to me often about racism and discrimination, anti-Black prejudice and antisemitism. One of my parents' heroes was Eleanor Roosevelt; my mother told me about Eleanor's part in establishing the Universal Declaration of Human Rights. My mother gave generously of her time and energy which she could have devoted more abundantly to her artwork, serving on the PTA, volunteering at Planned Parenthood and not-for-profit arts organizations, and campaigning for political candidates, roping in her skeptical daughters as assistants. My mother and I engaged in classic battles over unfinished meals and the world's hungry children. All these be-a-good-human sessions had an abiding influence on me. Not that my parents' conscientious cultivation of empathy and compassion precluded complaining, selfishness, arguments, gossip, jealousy, tantrums, evasiveness, and lies. But we did have aspirational ideals in accord with the fundamentals of tikkun olam, a Hebrew term that translates as "world repair" and that has been adapted from its kabbalistic origin and mystical meaning to refer to social responsibility and action, to acts of kindness and generosity, to working for the common good, to helping fix a broken world.

As a bookish girl, I loved that Jews were known as the "people of the book." I understood that my ancestors survived hate, discrimination, violence, conquest, dispossession, exile, enslavement, attempted protective assimilation, and genocide because their faith and core beliefs and identity were portable. Judaism resided within each person in stories, tenets, ideas, prayers, songs, and jokes; it lived on the scroll and the page. Jewish thought, commitment, and traditions could thrive anywhere and in many variations. Without religious instruction or inclination, I nonetheless found my way to a rather Talmudic life of study and analysis, to creating my own literary midrash, and living a life that would not have been available to me as a woman in Jewish worlds of the past in which only men were allowed to study.

Because we didn't belong to a temple, I would not have a bat mitzvah, so my do-it-yourself parents improvised a secular coming-of-age celebration for me, a surprise thirteenth-birthday party. My parents were avid party-throwers, and I was used to all the preparations and chaos leading up to gatherings of friends and family, but somehow all the preparatory work for this event was accomplished in secret. I was astonished to hear cars parking and car doors slamming on our quiet street on that warm, sunny July afternoon, and to see people streaming up the lawn to our front door. I don't remember much about the rest of that festive day, except that I received one gift that made me feel truly known, understood, and embraced: the Modern Library edition of *Lord Jim* by Joseph Conrad. My heart raced as I held that compact, well-designed volume. How did this family friend know that bookstruck me was covertly making my way through the classics? Soon after, another close friend of my parents gave me Virginia Woolf's *A Room of One's Own*, and my parents gave me Rachel Carson's *The Sea Around Us*, two endlessly resonant books that marked crucial paths.

I don't remember a single school reading assignment, but I do remember coming under the spell of the *Odyssey* and the *Iliad*. I read as many Kurt Vonnegut novels as I could get my hands on. *Slaughterhouse-Five* became one of my regular rereads. What cued me to Hermann Hesse? Something in the air. I got scolded when I was caught reading *Demian* in algebra class; I stayed up late to read *Steppenwolf* and *The Glass Bead Game*. I read Emily Dickinson, Walt Whitman, Allen Ginsberg, and Richard Brautigan. When I wasn't reading, I was listening to music. All these works of inquiry, art, and dissent whirled in my mind, phosphorescent and provoking.

During the two years I attended our city's one public high school the library was a haven. I darted in there whenever I could, and the librarian was kind, keeping her distance while keeping watch as I found a corner in which to read, worry, and plot between classes and bomb scares. Threatening phone calls and yanked fire alarms were routine, so we kept our coats on, our backpacks between our feet, always ready to evacuate the building. I kept a paperback handy, happy to read outside until the all-clear.

As in most high schools, there were factions; some of us elicited ire just by being our cynical, pissed-off selves. We were lucky then; no one brought guns to school. Switchblades flashed. I was stuck with a hat pin and lightly cut with a razor. Some guy flipped a lit cigarette at me, and it caught in my hair; a bloody tooth landed in my egg salad when a fight broke out in the cafeteria. Drugs were rampant; the administration's countermeasure was to padlock most of the bathrooms. That induced many of us to skip out early. The constant uproar was over race, war, and class. The stodgy old order and rigid curriculum clashed against the new consciousness. We were hormonal, angry, ill-informed, impatient, and arrogant. But we were also sincere, caring, focused on justice, and rightfully furious over pollution and other environmental atrocities, racism, nuclear weapons, sexism, outrageously harsh drug laws, and unwarranted police violence.

I was reading Eldridge Cleaver's *Soul on Ice*; Alan Paton's *Cry, the Beloved Country*; James Baldwin's

Another Country; Norman Mailer's *Armies of the Night*; Joan Didion's *Slouching Towards Bethlehem*; D. H. Lawrence's *Lady Chatterley's Lover*; Carlos Castaneda's *Journey to Ixtlan*; Vine Deloria Jr.'s *Custer Died for Your Sins: An Indian Manifesto*; and Quentin Bell's biography of Virginia Woolf, whose books I have read and reread. I read insatiably because I was angry, alienated, yearning, depressed, and determined to know more. I read to anchor myself to something larger and more meaningful, to a universe I could trust. I was rebellious and in retreat. I preferred my fledgling life of the mind to family and social interactions. My inner compass is oriented to solitary investigations. Marijuana stoked this inclination not only because it loosened the vise of my self-disgust but also because it turned everyday moments into adventures, enhancing experiences and reflections. My thoughts felt large and significant. I felt as though I was surrounded by metaphors, as though I was climbing the entwined vines stories generated.

As my father coaxed me into a more disciplined reading habit by having me write book reports to earn my allowance, I gave shape and direction to my voracious reading by assigning myself reading lists. I was curious about Russia because my mother's grandmother, her guiding light in a shattered childhood and my tiny great-grandmother, her gray hair in coiled braids, was from Odesa, while my mother's father was born near Kyiv, where her grandfather grew up. So, I decided to read Russia's literary giants, a worthy project that just so happened to coincide with a petty crime spree.

Shoplifting is a rite of passage for teens pushing back against authority, however ill-defined. Why I thought the modest stores on my hometown's struggling Main Street were fair game for pilfering, when I was fed, clothed, and sheltered by scrupulously honest parents is beyond reason. All I can say is that the impulse flowed from feeling powerless in a world where adults were hell-bent on destroying the biosphere, where racism was virulent and violent, where poverty afflicted working families, and where wars raged incoherently. This pseudo act of protest was also a high, of course, with its calculated risk-taking, criminal skill, and adrenalin rush. Since I looked like a harmless middle-class white girl and was always polite, I didn't alarm shopkeepers or salesclerks. I was able to flip through record albums at leisure before I snuck one or two beneath my long rust-colored wool coat and sauntered out.

One numbingly cold day I was in a small bookstore and gift shop. It smelled of scented candles and soaps and incense. Weavings and macramé hung on the walls and its shelves and tables displayed hand-crafted pottery and hand-blown glass along with an intriguing selection of books. Dostoevsky was my target, and a densely paged paperback edition of *The Idiot* was perfect for pocketing. I meandered a bit with my hidden prize and then headed for the door.

The shopkeeper stopped me, asking gently, "Did you want to pay for that?" My heart seized. I suddenly saw her in a heavenly beam of focusing light. Her hair was loosely gathered in a low, wispy knot. Her skirt was long, her earrings dangling. She looked sad, disappointed, weary, and kind. I could feel myself flush red. I extracted the book and held it out to her carefully, as though it would break. "Who's the idiot?" I asked ruefully, tremulously. Surprised, she laughed briefly, reluctantly. I really wanted the book; maybe she even wanted me to have it. My breath was trapped in my chest; my head throbbed. We stood caught in a momentous spell of mutual regard and inquiry. This edition, with its commanding mosaic portrait of a staring man with large, expressive, dark eyes, dark eyebrows raised philosophically, a dark, downturned moustache, cost all of 95 cents. Did I come up with a dollar and pay for it? Like an interrupted dream, the scene fades. I was in such an extreme state of mortification, my memory shut down. All I can say is that I did leave with the book, which I've read and reread, each time realizing how much I missed before. Each time I send gratitude to that kind shopkeeper. The book is with me still. The shop closed soon after I committed my unpunished crime.

***

As the regular school year ended and the summer I would turn sixteen began, I'd had enough of drugs. Set within a constellation of colleges and universities and just a meditative drive to Woodstock to the north and within reach of New York City to the south, Poughkeepsie was narcotics central, and for a cynical yet romantic young woman at once withdrawn and reckless and who could pass as someone a bit older, drugs in all forms were laughably easy to come by. I tried every available substance, put myself in serious danger, and began to feel suicidal. Finally, these perilous pursuits struck me as a wretched and ludicrous waste of time. I wanted to create things, read, and write. I didn't want to get hooked; I certainly didn't want to OD. People in my druggy circle had done both. I wanted to be strong and healthy and free. The more messed up you got, the more endangered your precious privacy became as adults meddled, slung useless platitudes, and tried to boss you around. I knew how profoundly fortunate I was to not have become helplessly addicted and to have a sanctuary in which I could heal myself. The drugs then were not as potently and cruelly ensnaring as they are now. Users had a fighting chance.

I decided I had to quit cold and do a deep cleanse. No one knew the full extent of my drug use, wildness, or brushes with disaster, and I offered only the vaguest explanation for my own private rehab. I suppose my parents were so relieved that I was staying home they didn't want to rile me. I started sleeping on the porch that my father would later turn into my mother's studio, eating wholesomely, remaining in solitude as much as possible, and practicing intensive book therapy. I read and read and read, slowly lifting myself out of despondency, fear, shame, and hopelessness. My parents belonged to the Book of the Month Club, so we had James Michener, Barbara Tuchman, John Cheever, John Updike, and Philip Roth on hand. I also read Edith Wharton, Ernest Hemingway, F. Scott Fitzgerald, William Faulkner, John Fowles, Thomas Pynchon, and Aleksandr Solzhenitsyn. I felt rinsed, spun, infused, renewed, and determined. I realized that this new me needed to attend a new school.

Although adults repeatedly told me that I was not living up to my potential, the shock of my failing two tenth-grade classes was seismic. Those appalling F's were the result of my skipping afternoon classes to get away from the chaos, find a bathroom, and smoke weed. So, I was confident in the deal I offered my worried parents, who were treating me as cautiously as one does a cornered wild beast. I promised that I would attend summer school and bring my grades back up if they could figure out how to send me to the local private day school. This small John Dewey-style institution had just extended its kindergarten-through-eighth-grade program to include four years of high school since many students there didn't want to attend the public high school I was hoping to escape. I'd been told that it was a perfect place for kids like me. There were no grades, and independence and creativity were encouraged.

On a breezy sunny day that seemed designed for daring, I decided to go see for myself. I skipped school and rode my bike outside the city limits to the edge of the Vassar College campus. There sat the large one-story day school like an island in a sea of grass backed by sheltering woods. I walked through the unlocked door into the lobby uninvited, without an appointment or permission. How casual and spontaneous life was then. A tall, calm woman came out of the front office and asked if she could help me. Clearly, I should have been in class somewhere, but she didn't mention my truancy. I gamely explained that I was hoping to look around, that I was interested in attending. I gazed out into the school's large open space, called the Big Room, while she went in search of a student who could give me a tour. She returned with a lanky, long-haired, and bemused high school senior who offered laconic, vaguely encouraging commentary as we walked through the school. I was impressed. Radiant with natural light, this was a modern variation on the one-room schoolhouse, with moveable bookcases marking off space for classes and students of all ages sitting on the floor. The contrast to the public high school with its long, echoing hallways and cage-like classrooms was visceral.

My guide delivered me back to the front office and loped away. I planned to thank the kind administrator who so graciously welcomed me and get back on my bike. Instead, she asked if I wanted to speak to the director. I was stunned. Frightened. This was supposed to be a guerrilla operation; I had planned to make a quick getaway. But I couldn't say no. I was ushered into a comfortable sunny office full of books and an old globe. The director, bearded and relaxed, stood, greeted me warmly, and settled back into his leather chair, crossing his legs, lighting a pipe, and keeping his bright, inquisitive eyes on mine.

I sat on the edge of my seat, tense and cautious. But when he asked why I was there, I took a breath and came clean, telling this good patient man how frustrated I was with all the turmoil at the public high school. I confessed my frequent absences and my worry about the future. I nearly levitated when he asked me what I was reading and what I was interested in. I named a slew of books and muttered something vague about wanting to be creative. Rather than shift to practical matters, the director leaned back and posed some trippy questions, one about time and traveling in a spaceship. I don't recall the details, but whatever answer I came up with based on hazy physics and a cosmic inclination seemed to please him. I knew he was trying to get a sense of how I thought, of how receptive I was to new ideas, to new challenges. I felt that we were in accord, that I belonged at his school, and I told him so. I also admitted that my parents had no idea I was there or that I was even thinking about trying to enroll. I confessed that I wasn't sure we could afford the tuition.

He remained contemplative, pipe smoke rising in a slow, lazy blue plume. He stood and shook my hand at the conclusion of our conversation. Feeling like a lost child in a fairy tale lucking upon a wise and gracious king, I struggled to keep it together as I thanked the generous director for his time, the etiquette my mother drilled into me surfacing even in the midst of this act of defiance. But I was shaking by the time I reached my bike. And my brain was on fire. I had to convince my parents that it was imperative for me to secure refuge in this oasis. Ultimately, that small progressive school saved my sanity and my life.

As with public school, I have no recollection of any English classes at this capacious place for learning. According to the teacher reports—lengthy disquisitions about their students' participation in class in lieu of grades—I did take a poetry class and one on surrealism. The math instruction was far more conceptual than the standard fare; we talked about Schrödinger and the cat. I reveled in the biology and chemistry courses; the lab was well-equipped, and the women teachers were smart and lively. The school had dark rooms, and I devoted myself to black-and-white photography. All this hands-on action was exactly what I needed; lots of doing, not sitting, bored and restless, in rote classes. The school also had an all-ages coed soccer team and a folk-dancing troupe. The older students made lunches for everyone; we even collected sap from the surrounding maple trees and made maple syrup. All these endeavors were balms to my spirit. But the most miraculous gift was the weaving studio, the domain of Ailsa Hubner, who was skilled in the old ways and busy restoring large nineteenth-century looms.

The line-by-lineness of weaving evokes the act of reading. Each throw of the weft-bearing boat shuttle between the warp threads opened by pressing the treadles which lifted the shaft which held the heddles through which the warp was threaded added a line to the cloth or tapestry, added a sentence to the threaded story. With each gliding passage of the shuttle and each pull of the batten, the weaver adds to an emerging scene, image, conversation, thought, memory, feeling. Thread, yarn, and cloth have long been associated with storytelling. A yarn is a tale; one spins a story. A storyteller connects the threads or weaves a tale or knits story lines together. Weavings and stories are made of patterns. Word by word, thread by thread, an idea, an impression, a character, a world takes shape. A loom is a metronome, a clock, a percussive instrument, a tool for meditation. Hand, eye, and mind are deeply engaged, transporting the weaver, the contemplative, the tale-builder beyond the boundaries and shortcomings of the self, the everyday. The weaver, the dreamer, the storyteller sways back and forth on the bench, hands on the bar like a ship's tiller, the steady motion like rowing or davening or playing the piano or writing at a keyboard. There's a rhythm to the back-and-forth of weaving and a rhythm to the line-by-line, page-by-page procession the reader performs. These are acts of coordination, skill, and transcendence. Each casts a spell, and each creates raiment for the body or the soul.

* * *

Is the sense of beauty innate? An aspect of sentience? Is passionate appreciation for Earth's vibrant spectrum of life-forms, colors, infinite patterns and textures, scents and sounds a trait that evolved to prompt human beings to value their surroundings? If only that were true for more of us in more places over more time. If only we protected living treasures as expertly and passionately as we conserve and secure works of art. Paintings by haloed artists are auctioned for astronomical sums, while we squabble over attempts to preserve a species, a forest, a wetland, a prairie, a river, an ocean. Life itself.

The Hudson Valley is a verdant, sensuous place. The Mahicans (or Mohicans) knew the river as the Mahicannituck; the Lenape called it the Shatemuc, which translates in English as "the river that flows both ways" or "great waters in constant motion," names that reflect how, for much of its run, it's a tidal estuary that reverses its north-south flow with the tides. The hills, meadows, rounded old mountains, deep forests, rampant wildflowers, grasses, fruit trees, evergreens, maples, oaks, and beeches are vibrant and entrancing. My mother's exquisite incised-ink paintings were inspired by the Shawangunk and Catskill mountains, birch trees, Queen Anne's lace, anemones, and irises. The valley's natural wonders spoke to young me; I was an "earth ecstatic," to use Diane Ackerman's term. Once I had my driver's license and was able to explore further from home on my own, I became even more enthralled by the intricacy of existence. I would gaze at the back-and-forth river, seeing its oppositional currents as embodiments of my own concurrent doubts and convictions, questions and reversals, the perpetual back-and-forth between hope and despair. My simultaneous angst and nature-rapture fed a key tributary of my river of reading.

The most ardent and intentional writers observe the world around them and ask what is altered, what is lost, and what holds fast. They help us see where we've been and who we've been, who we are and who we may become. Writers attuned to the symbiotic entanglements and circle dances of nature describe with precision and wonder what it feels like to walk through Yeats' "bee-loud glade," or an old-growth forest striated with shadows and thrumming with life. But how many of us now experience such vibrant places? Most humans can't even see the stars at night, so brightly illuminated are our massive metropolises. The songs of birds and whales are drowned out and quiet itself is endangered by the perpetual cacophony of our machines. Will lyrical descriptions of the wild or the night sky become mere symbols, literary contrivances no longer connected to living entities and sensuous experience? Will earthly splendor be reduced to streaming images under glass?

Robert Finch and John Elder, editors of the Norton anthology *Nature Writing: The Tradition in English*, write in their introduction that "the landscape of nature writing ... offers a consoling largeness ... It allows for a vision of wholeness, informed by the natural sciences but attuned to the human and spiritual meanings of our earth and the living communities that it sustains. And it gives access to the unforgettable voices of men and women, who, in paying attention to the vivid, dynamic outer world, have also clarified our own sense of identity and purpose." While the battle between burgeoning corporations and stalwart river defenders, including Pete Seeger with his sloop *Clearwater*, was raging over the unconscionable polluting of the Hudson, I read Henry David Thoreau, that magnet for questing young people, that trail-marking chronicler and champion of the living world, community, and independent thought. As a daughter of an artist and an electrical engineer, I easily appreciated the balance of art and science in nature writing's union of lyricism and fact. Writers attuned to ecological wonders and ethical considerations have been essential in awakening us to the interconnectivity and vulnerability of life, and to the catastrophic consequences of our reliance on fossil fuels and toxic chemicals.

From Thoreau I turned to Henry Beston's *The Outermost House*, following a visit to its setting, Cape Cod, and then on to John Burroughs, John Muir, and Aldo Leopold. I was captivated by the irascible renegade Edward Abbey, whose *Desert Solitaire* I've reread at different junctures in my life. I was spellbound by Annie Dillard's *Pilgrim at Tinker Creek*, and I have followed Dillard through all her subsequent nature-illuminating, creatively philosophical books.

The need for gripping books that elucidate the impact of our marauding species' decimation of the living world and the acceleration of climate change has increased exponentially in our lifetimes. As Bill McKibben, whose civic-minded books include *The End of Nature*, the first title to explain global warming to the reading public back in 1989, writes in his defining anthology, *American Earth: Environmental Writing since Thoreau*, environmental writing "subsumes and moves beyond nature writing, seeking answers as well as consolation, embracing controversy, sometimes sounding an alarm."

The work of writers on the axis between science and literature is essential to our understanding the dynamism of our planet and to figuring out how to live more in harmony with the rest of life on Earth and find ways to preserve life rather than decimate it. Since my earliest raptures over nature's power, largesse, and beauty, I've been enthralled by and grateful to writers who cast light on the intricate web of life and all that threatens it, including Diane Ackerman, Charles Bowden, Wade Davis, Gretel Ehrlich, Jane Goodall, Linda Hogan, Elizabeth Kolbert, J. Drew Lanham, Barry Lopez, Helen Macdonald, Lydia Millet, Sy Montgomery, Mary Oliver, Annie Proulx, David Rothenberg, Leslie Marmon Silko, Carl Safina, Rebecca Solnit, Terry Tempest Williams, and Edward O. Wilson.

Nature-focused writers tell us that we must not lose sight of the fact that we are animals, that we need clean air, fresh water, healthy food, and shelter. We need every thread in the vast and vastly intricate web of life to be intact. We cannot rely on our built infrastructure and ever-bossier machines, no matter how wedded we are to electricity, devices, search engines, and vehicles. Our fossil-fuel-powered grid has given us superpowers that enable us to thrive and destroy, and we seem determined to trash a living world of miraculous complexity, balance, beauty, and adaptability. The fact that evolution created a species capable of increasing the glory of life and demolishing it is a paradox of endless puzzlement and tragedy.

In *Banzeiro Òkòtó: The Amazon as the Center of the World*, Brazilian journalist Eliane Brum chronicles her reasons for leaving the conveniences and comfort of São Paulo to immerse herself in the crisis that is undermining the planet-sustaining Amazon. She describes her river journey: "Its gentle christening aside, the little river of Riozinho is wild. Tree trunks formed caves atop the water, a pair of giant otters dove about right in front of us, and thousands, perhaps millions, of yellow butterflies kept us company on our labyrinthine course. It seemed we had been swallowed up into some unknown dimension in a distracted blink of the eye. I felt like I was diving deeper and deeper into Earth. A certainty burned between my breasts the whole time, a certainty that no matter how well I might write, I would be unable to capture the dimension of what I saw and lived."

Later Brum writes about reading "a scientific article about butterflies in the Amazon. In various parts of the rainforest, they are losing their color. They are no longer yellow, blue, red, orange, green, pink, purple ... but brown and gray. Butterflies also want to survive and so are adapting to the end of the world, mimicking the ash gray of the incinerated forest and the concrete gray encasing Earth like a straitjacket, eventually asphyxiating all life."

Though we are failing to protect the wild, when we think of preservation, we tend to focus on areas not yet despoiled, but nature is all-encompassing. Nothing we humans create, from maps to condominiums to cell phones to ocean liners are separate from nature. We must save what wilderness we have left—the Amazon is essential to earthly life—and we must also cherish and protect nature as we find it on city streets, high-raise balconies, mall parking lots, parks and play-grounds, suburban yards, and interstate rest stops.

I am entranced by Vs of geese flying over bumper-to-bumper expressway traffic, flower-eating deer, squirrels arcing across small backyards, little eager sparrows filtering through a chain-link fence like stunt pilots, the house cat in the window, the dog at the door, and a pair of mourning doves perched on an electrical cable above the alley, turning rosy as they watch the sun go down. Life is manifold, complex, miraculous, and precious, and our brainy, restless, and voracious species is but one clan in the vast and diverse family of Earth. Ever since I first read about pollution, endan-gered whales, clear-cut logging, and global warming, I've been distraught. I fear that humankind's phenom-enal capacity for adaptation, like that of the Amazon butterflies, means that we won't act to halt the collapse of biodiversity, the loss of forests, the poisoning and acidification of the warming oceans. We'll just shift our alliance wholly to the virtual world, giving up the richness of our senses at work in the full dimensionality of real life. As it is, I find myself so lashed to the screen that when I do go outside, I'm dizzy with the press and swirl of wind, the warmth of sunlight, the touch of rain, surround sound, and waves of scent, the grand dance of everything in motion.

I do find hope in how ardently and wisely scientists, historians, journalists, naturalists, poets, fiction writers, and memoirists write about nature and our place within the whole. Writers in the know urge us not to succumb to the gray, the diminishment, the muting, the loss, the loneliness we'll face as beings who have squandered miracles. All I seem able to do consistently is share my belief in stories that illuminate the wonders of the biosphere. I hope that by urging others to read what I'm reading they will also feel grateful for life and compelled to help protect its grandeur, vitality, and munificence.

Books can be springboards for social change, offering arguments for change and charting the way forward. But do books reach beyond the spheres of already concerned readers? Can books truly help propel the vast sea change we need to slow the worst fallout from climate change? In *We Loved It All*, Lydia Millet writes, "Storytelling will never be the same as action. But action depends on a perception of possibility, which only arises from the tales we tell ourselves."

"We must alter what it means to be human in our era," writes Eliane Brum. We've performed radical advances before, and books are often the catalyst for justice and preservation. Books elucidate our intricate connection to other humans and other living entities by stoking our imagination, our instinct for self-preservation, and—one hopes—our empathy. Books clarify the challenges we face and how we can help enact necessary progress in attitude and action.

The Blue River, a Tributary

What works of art testify to is the presence in this world of consciousness, consciousness of many extraordinary kinds ... It is not the writer's awareness I am speaking of but the awareness he or she makes. For that is what fine writing does: it creates a unique verbal consciousness.

—William Gass

... The good reader is one who has imagination, memory, a dictionary, and some artistic sense.

—Vladimir Nabokov

The plan was for me to drive the family car, an olive-brown, low-to-the-ground, many-miled Buick Skylark that looked more amphibian than avian, from Poughkeepsie to Kansas City, where I would sell it and live off the proceeds. It was a fine old American ride, speedy and sturdy, even after I ripped out the muffler while inching over a sandy, tree-root-laddered stretch of campground on Cape Cod. My friend and I, all of eighteen years old, sunburned and giddy, managed to pick up and spear the hot metal pipe through the open backdoor window and across the backseat, and then lurch and roar our way to a gas station. Later we walked barefoot to the tip of the peninsula, in awe of the smashing, crisscrossing waves. Something neatly sliced open the sole of one foot. A shell, a glass shard? I plunged my aching, bleeding foot in the cold salty ocean repeatedly, certain that would cleanse the wound. But as my friend and I headed West to attend the Kansas City Art Institute, we hadn't gone any farther than Harrisburg, Pennsylvania, when we had to stop because red lines were mapping my leg like highways to hell.

The emergency room doctor was appalled at my recklessness—he had no idea. After an unplanned night in a cheap motel where I soaked my infected leg in Epsom salts and began taking antibiotics, we continued on our way, with me propping my swollen leg up on the dashboard or through the open window, air whooshing between my toes. The Skylark had no air conditioning, and the heat was broiling. We were sweating so much we decided to take off our drenched shirts and bras, figuring that no one would see that we were topless as we flew by at eighty-five miles per hour.

Once we arrived on the small campus, I realized there was no way for me, an overwhelmed freshman in a dorm with only one hallway phone, to sell this old car on my own in a strange city. One of the maintenance crew, a kind country gent bemused by the hubris of art students from points East and West, took charge and eventually handed me $750. Disastrously less than we expected. My parents had imagined that I would get enough for the car to live on for the school year. This was crucial because they were not around to help me. My father had landed the most coveted of IBM assignments: two years in Paris.

He and my mother were ecstatic. For them, this was beyond a dream come true. But my fifteen-year-old sister, a country girl mad for horses, was aghast. Not only had I left her alone with my parents, but she also dreaded living in a big foreign city without knowing the language. Everyone found it incongruous

that while my family was living overseas in a legendary art mecca, I was counting pennies in Missouri. But
I was more than ready to be on my own, and IBM paid
the airfare for two family visits a year. This inspired
my French and Americans-in-Paris reading excursion
during my art-school years that ultimately encom-
passed Guillaume Apollinaire, Honoré de Balzac,
Charles Baudelaire, Jean Cocteau, Marguerite Duras,
M. F. K. Fisher, F. Scott Fitzgerald, Janet Flanner,
Ernest Hemingway, Henry Miller, Anaïs Nin, Marcel
Proust, Arthur Rimbaud, George Sand, Gertrude
Stein, and Émile Zola.

During one of my extended stays, my father
brought us along on a business trip to the Scottish
town of Greenock, situated where the River Clyde
opens out into the Firth of Clyde. There sprawled an
enormous IBM plant, a high-tech complex that was
eventually abandoned and, years later, demolished.
We stayed further up the coast in Gourock, where it
was damp, chilly, and draped with gray clouds like
sheets over furniture. The waterfront was scruffy
with graffiti writhing across cement barriers; the

pier spiked with towering cranes as fishing boats and industrial ships pulled at their anchors. But I was also dwelling in the fecund, butterflied, spellbound Colombian village of Macondo: I was reading Gabriel García Márquez's *One Hundred Years of Solitude*. I can still slip into that particular heady duality in which I hovered between two evocatively mysterious realms in different hemispheres and climes, defined by different mythologies and languages—one experienced viscerally, the other through words—but both wholly alive and redolent with nature's humbling grandeur and epic human longing.

In art school I was surrounded by creative people for whom words were not their chosen mode of creative expression. Not that many weren't witty, dramatic, even outlandish in conversation. Many were captivating taletellers and lancing social commentators, and some were passionate readers. But the visual dominated their perceptions. They understood perspective and spatial dimensions down to their bones. They could draw, paint, sculpt, build, and design with far more skill and certainty than I, but many balked when they had to write papers for our liberal arts classes. The doubly gifted—visual artists who also read and wrote—were stars, their notebooks brimming with words and images, their studio spaces lined with books and art materials. I wasn't doubly gifted; I was doubly obsessed. For all the long hours I spent at the studio, I still read at length, too. When I first heard about the Kansas City Art Institute, I assumed it was in Kansas, of which I knew little beyond the movie *The Wizard of Oz*. Of Missouri, where I docked, except for a hazy sense of St. Louis as a Mississippi River city acquired through blues, jazz, and another Judy Garland movie, I knew nothing.

Students from New York, Boston, Pennsylvania, Cleveland, Michigan, Chicago, Indiana, Colorado, Oklahoma, Nebraska, California, and Oregon, if memory serves, convened on the compact campus, a haven for young outliers. But beyond the quad, the studio buildings, and the border fences and hedges, cultures clashed. I'd never been called a Yankee before. Nor told to slow down because I was talking so darn fast, they couldn't understand a single word

I was saying. I'd never been half-asked, half-told so often that Jews were a race, right? "Like the Blacks?"

My friend and I chose this small art institute in the, to us, enigmatic Midwest because it had textile and glass departments. We emerged from our hands-on day school versed in and enamored of traditional crafts, and we dreamt of using them as vehicles for artistic expression. I was entranced by the works of fiber artists Anni Albers, Sheila Hicks, and Lenore Tawney. My friend was intent on developing her glass-blowing skills. But after we were accepted, both programs were shut down. I gave myself over to the unpredictable and consuming challenges of the Foundation program and hoped for inspiration regarding my major. One assignment required us to dig up, preserve, and draw an eight-inch square of earth, a task requiring resourcefulness of many kinds. That was the point. After we managed to borrow shovels and trowels to make our hacking excavations, I found my little table-top mesa of Missouri soil, a dirt layer cake, an earthy lesson in microcosms and fractals. During another session, I made enormous drawings by tracing life-sized shadows on white paper pinned to the walls.

In a notebook from that pivotal year, I find that I was still not using capital letters and that I come across as surprisingly clear-eyed and assured, given my memories of rampant insecurity and mortifying failures. Here are accounts of performance pieces I don't remember coming up with or enacting. Appraisals of art school social dynamics and frustrations with my own struggles. I wrote: "i should work harder." A mantra that subsequently appeared in every notebook I've ever kept.

After talking with the dean, herself a weaver, and being assured that eventually I could work with materials of my choosing, including fiber, I decided that the sculpture department was a good match. This was the kingdom of Dale Eldred, a world-traveling sculptor who worked on a spectacular scale with unusual materials to capture the dazzle and power of light. The churning, contradictory, intimating, sometimes dangerous goings-on in Eldred's muscular arena were deeply instructive and expansive.

I learned to ignore my fear of dismemberment and enjoy using the roaring table saws and whining drill presses in the wood shop, wearing goggles and steel-toed work boots and logging so many sawdusty hours I had an Ovidesque dream in which my flesh was metamorphosing into wood. I also dreamed that in order to write, I had to climb up and jump on the towering keys of a giant typewriter.

The atavistic metal-casting sessions were cause for ceremony and inebriation. The flames, the molten steel poured from a suspended, spouted cauldron, the chains and pulleys, the clamor and leaping shadows and gusts of heat—all transformed the work-a-day studio building into a temple enshrining expression, transformation, and risk. All our cultural trappings fell away as the evening turned primal. It was a battle against the elements: gravity, friction, heat, blades, hammers, tongs, toxic chemicals, competition, nausea, sexual desire. Men outnumbered women and some of the guys were older and tougher, military veterans who sculpted with chainsaws and acetylene torches. Big, assertive works threatened to overpower the fine and the subtle, but hard work earned credibility and there are many ways to be tough and committed.

It was exhilarating and exhausting, infuriating and discouraging. I was forever regretting things I said and left unsaid, things I did and didn't do. I wanted to revise, to edit, to have a "take two." I kept most of my angst to myself, and I always had a ready refuge: I always had books. Back in my apartment, I slipped out of the cage of my conflicted self and into meticulously crafted language, refined thoughts, articulated feelings, richly informed visions, and stories illuminating nature's glory and human per-plexity. Immersions in books helped me return to the fray strengthened, a bit more cued to the imprint of the past upon the present, the commonality of fear and longing, impulses devious and altruistic. I could shift my focus from myself to others, understanding that they, too, might be beset, bewildered, anxious, resentful, lost. Perspective and relativity were guiding principles affirmed and deepened by each good book.

We did things that schools would never allow now, like ride in the back of open-bed trucks to an old, defunct quarry and gather rocks, riding back at sunset sunstruck, dirty, tired, and exultant, tossed around among our potentially bone-crushing harvest. The assignment was for each of us to build a stone sculpture on the lawn surrounding the sculpture building. The only things I had built up to at that point were frames for weaving small tapestries. My handy engineer father could fix everything from cars to washing machines; he also built furniture and cabinets. The many traits I inherited from him did not include his facility with tools and straight lines, his technical knowhow, or his mathematical fluency. But I've always been intrigued by stones and their compression of time and matter, their shapes, textures, colors, and solidity.

I collect stones and find comfort in holding them: there's an array of stones on my desk as I write, pocketed from various places, many found near bodies of water. I've always loved the dry stacked stone walls traversing the woods of the Hudson Valley. The walls flow in sync with the contour of the rising and falling land, curving and banking like a stone stream, like staffs of musical notes, like long, intricate scrolls, each stone a word, each line a sentence. Stones were abundant because this is glacial terrain packed with boulders and rocks dragged from afar. Before the settlers' conquest, the region's Indigenous communities created stone barriers, mounds, markings, and monuments. Many of the remaining puzzle-piece balancing acts are the work of early arriving white colonists, while the larger efforts requiring more extensive and painstaking labor were constructed by enslaved artisans.

Stone walls still run for thousands of miles in eastern New York and New England, just as they do in England, which inspired artist and seeming magician Andy Goldsworthy to create two celebrated stone walls on the rolling grounds of the Storm King Art Center, in Cornwall, New York, overlooking the Hudson River. Goldsworthy works with nature in nature, creating elegant sculptures of breathtaking balance and exquisite patterns. These subtle, ephemeral, one would think impossible works of stones, sticks, leaves, stalks, ice, and sand, constructions vulnerable to sun, wind, storms, tides, and time, remind us to look more carefully at the living world and consider more deeply our place within the fine mesh of life. In *Stone*, Goldsworthy observes, "A stone is one and many stones at the same time—it changes from day to day, season to season."

My stone structure was a clumsy riff on ancient shrines I found in library books about traditional architecture in Africa, India, and Asia. Almost pineapple-shaped and held together with cement laboriously mixed by hand and heavily applied, the acidic chemicals no one warned me about leaching through my flimsy gloves, it had a rocky floor and solid curving walls topped with pointy stones forming a spiky crown. The entrance was roughly oval. Once inside on the jagged floor, you could look up at a rock-rimmed patch of sky. Punishing to build, it was solid, crude, strange, and brash, a private monument to toughing it out, a clunky little fort with a vibe at once willful and contemplative.

Outside of assignments, my approach to making sculpture began to tilt toward the linear. I built a tall ladder of carved and notched wood with rungs too eccentrically shaped to stand on. I assembled works out of many small pieces of wood. Some formed irregularly latticed enclosures, corrals for invisible entities; others lay flat like mosaics. I created an installation piece for which I made a rag rug and a big, heavy quilt with two shiny, lacy, crinoline-puffed little-girl dresses appliquéd at the center, the sort my mother loved to see us in, with our little white gloves and shiny Mary Janes. Dreadful throw-back dresses I loathed for being itchy, annoying, and ridiculous. The gloves were ludicrous, too, ghosts from an earlier era and instantly soiled. I made a piece out of an old ironing board accompanied by a large papier-mâché figure. I was teased about my low skill "technologies" as the guys put it: my use of wire and thread to connect things, my use of found objects. The sculpture studio was dusty, oily, loud, and hectic. I began to work in my apartment, where I gravitated inexorably toward paper and colored pencils, making densely patterned drawings, the texture and details tiptoeing towards letters and words. I always snuck back to where I was happiest, the pages of books.

Liberal arts courses were required. Some were standard college survey courses, but we also took art history courses and literature courses taught by professors following their passions. One had us reading fiction by women writers, including, to my profound pleasure, Virginia Woolf. Hal Wert, an expert on Japanese culture, art, and literature, ushered us into what was for me an entirely new world. We read *The Tale of Genji* and works by Yasunari Kawabata and Kobo Abé, whose *The Woman in the Dunes*, the novel and the film—a surreal, claustrophobic, Sisyphean, and Kafkaesque tale of entrapment and enslavement, desperation and surrender—has haunted me ever since.

We were sitting outside on the grass in an arc facing the professor who was stretched out on his side. His thick thatch of dark hair was finger-raked, so, too, his wild, dark beard. His eyes gleamed behind smudged glasses; his white button-down shirt was rumpled. James Thweatt, Jr. was teaching an Irish literature course, reciting from memory and with ardor poems and long passages from epic tales. He fully inhabited the lyrics and mythology of Ireland, which clearly sustained him. He was handing us the torch, and it was electrifying. I'd never heard of the ancient epic, the *Táin Bó Cúailng*. We were reading a translation by the Irish poet Thomas Kinsella, and I was impressed by the tale's strong women, beginning with Medb of Cruachan in the opening section, "Pillow Talk." How remarkable for a story of war to begin with a royal couple conversing in the royal bed, especially since they are decidedly not exchanging endearments or confidences or flirtatious banter as a prelude to lovemaking.

"It struck me," Ailill said, "how much better off you are today than the day I married you." Medb disagrees. She reminds him that she is "the highest and haughtiest" daughter of the "high king of Ireland," besting her five sisters "in grace and giving and battle and warlike combat." She brags about all the soldiers she commands and the province she rules. What's more, she says, "I thrive, myself, on all kinds of trouble." She seems to flatter him when she assures him that he is "the kind of man" she wanted, but then says, "for you're a kept man." So much for repose. The competition is on. All their possessions are "brought out," from cookware to jewels and livestock. When they find that Ailill has a bull greater than any in Medb's herd, she is quick to send an offer to a man in Ulster who has an even mightier bull, offering him "fifty yearly heifers," land, a chariot, and "my own friendly thighs on top of that" in exchange for borrowing or renting his bull for a year. Misunderstandings and rumors quickly lead to war; the involvement of the warrior hero, Cú Chulainn; and the intervention of goddesses, including one who inflicts harsh "pangs" on the men of Ulster in retribution for a confrontation during which a king of Ulster forced her to race her chariot while in labor with twins. This word-besotted teacher then guided us to Yeats and James Joyce, bestowing gifts of endless resonance.

***

The car-sale money went quickly; I had to find a job. The dean was immensely kind, hiring me to work in her office even though I was flagrantly unqualified. I was also assigned the work-study task of sweeping out the design department building early each morning. This was a plum gig since it was the cleanest of the studios. At daybreak I wielded a great-big broom and amassed a mountain of cigarette butts and ashes, pencil shavings, eraser dust, and scraps and slivers of paper and cardboard.

But these humble positions did not pay enough. The school job board delivered me to a Western Auto on a rundown stretch of Main Street. There I stocked the shelves and helped customers, mostly guys with grease in the creases of their hands and dirt under their fingernails. I looked up air and oil filter numbers in big oil-slippery catalogs, then searched the shelves of the behind-the-counter library. I rode my bike to the store, which did sell bike parts and bicycle flat-tire repair kits, dressed in my art-girl thrift-store finery: funky shirts and jeans and work boots, all shockingly boyish in contrast with the prevailing feminine style of that place and time. A New York Jew with cropped curly brown hair, scant make-up, and glasses who talked too fast, worked too hard, and did not flirt, I was an anomaly. My boss, a solid, short, mustached, regular-looking, middle-of-the-country white guy who revealed a touch of rebelliousness by driving a motorcycle to work, hired me, as he later unabashedly explained, because he assumed I was smart, and because he was sure that no one would find me attractive enough to waste time chatting me up or harassing me. We came to appreciate each other's frankness and sardonic senses of humor and enjoyed working together. But he was dead-wrong about how the customers treated me.

I was glad to be busy. There was no time to obsess over my failings or compulsively analyze my relationships. I was on my feet talking to strangers, stocking shelves, handling cash, credit cards, phone calls, and questions about everything from car parts to garden hoses. This down-to-earth job coincided with my reading Samuel Beckett's novels. I found *Molloy*, *Murphy*, and *Watt* hilarious, ludicrous, and poignant in their mirroring of human befuddlement. The cadence of the prose, the characters and their strange predicaments and existential conundrums are perfect embodiments of the absurdity and nobility of our struggles with the most basic aspects of existence.

My mood swings were intense. On one of many days when everything felt off-kilter and pointless, I wrote, "I don't know anything. I can't decide what to read because no one I see reads." I'm sure this lasted but a moment. I could not function without books, perhaps to an alarming degree; I even fretted about what I referred to as my "drug-reading." Not only did I retreat into books to avoid dealing with conflicts, but I also often found ordinary life tedious in comparison. "I'd rather be reading" was not always a healthy mantra.

Kansas City is hilly and green, and I took long moody walks with notebook and pen in pocket, a 35mm camera hanging from my shoulder. This bluesy jazz town is watered by the Blue River, curving its way to the much larger Missouri River through downtown. But of more interest to me was one of the Blue's three tributaries, Brush Creek, which runs along the art school campus and the neighboring Nelson-Atkins Museum of Art down the hill to the showplace Country Club Plaza and beyond to neighborhoods far more humble. This once free-flowing creek named for the plants that festooned its banks was paved and boxed in the 1930s to help prevent flooding (and, some rumors contend, to hide bodies), but containment is a fantasy. Heavy rains caused a catastrophic flash flood while I was there, a clamorous uprising in which the creek rampaged over its hard-edged prison to wreak havoc in the city, quickly filling streets, stranding people in their cars, smashing glass storefronts, and stealing two dozen human lives. Stringy, slimy debris, mud, sludge, downed branches, and shredded leaves were strewn all over the slowly draining streets and sidewalks and lawns. Waterlogged cars were piled up and crushed, dragged into buildings, and rolled, while below in flooded underground parking garages they bobbed like capsized boats.

Before the flood, when I wandered along brooding Brush Creek, I came across chance assemblages of bent-up shopping carts, busted chairs and crates, bottles and cans, mangled dolls, sticks, garbage, and muck pressed helter-skelter against the rectangular pillars of the overpasses, creating ripples in the otherwise uniform flow of the captive creek. Along its concrete banks was a forgotten underworld of abandoned houses with doors hanging open and crooked, aslant window blinds, encrusted dishes, mildewing furniture and rotting carpets, rusting fixtures, warping shelves and floors, draping cobwebs. Each room an incoherent story of life interrupted, of private disasters. Years later, Dale Eldred, my former professor and a global artist of mythic depths devoted to working audaciously with elemental forces, lost his studio, which contained his phenomenal personal library and many artworks, to fire. Soon thereafter, the city was flooded yet again, and Eldred lost his life at age 59, while trying to save valuable equipment from the rising river waters.

Money was tight; I had to be inventive about art supplies and I had to have books. The literature courses were exciting but not nearly enough. I found my way to Stanley Elkin, whose tenderly satirical cross-country saga, *The Franchiser*, granted me new keys to the country, especially the Midwest. I mention in a journal that I was reading Thomas Mann's *Faust*, a wellspring for so many works, including the novels of William Gaddis. Gaddis's mammoth debut, *The Recognitions*, a Faustian drama of art at its purest and as a corrupted commodity, chimed with my dilemma over the legitimacy of my own creative efforts and thoughts about originality, authenticity, and survival. As I worked in the studio, I could never shake free from the perfectly reasonable recognition of how anemic my work was compared to that of my more accomplished peers, let alone the masters. Why do it? Why not devote one's attention to true art? Art that would nurture, not defeat me.

Reading demanding books was far easier for me than facing the abrading demands of everyday life. I exhausted myself with worry; reading was the anti-dote. I don't remember anyone being interested in my literary obsession. Books were name-dropped in conversations, but I didn't chronicle any in-depth book conversations in my journals, and I don't recall any, while I do remember passionate exchanges about art, music, movies, and politics. I can't say that I really minded that my river-of-books voyage was solo; it was a transfixing and steadying solitude.

***

Through the art-school grapevine I heard that jobs were open at the Linda Hall Library, a world-renowned private science, technology, and engineering research facility adjacent to the nearby campus of the University of Missouri at Kansas City. Herbert Hall made his fortune exporting grain and he and his wife, Linda, dedicated philanthropists, left a six-million-dollar bequest for "a free public library for the use of the people of Kansas City and the public generally." Named in tribute to Linda and located on their fourteen-acre estate, the library was housed in their Georgian mansion when it opened in 1946. As the collection grew, a new building was added in 1956 and a new wing in 1965, which required the razing of the mansion. Additional extensions followed as it became the "largest independently funded public library of its kind in North America" and "among the largest science libraries in the world," as stated on the library website. In accordance with the Halls' stipulations, the property was planted with three hundred trees of different species from all around the world, thus creating a living library and sylvan refuge.

Linda Hall Library is elegant and spacious, its above-ground floors bathed in leafy light. As a closed-stack operation, most of its treasures are below ground where a subterranean minimum-wage crew retrieved materials for patrons, then reshelved the returned periodicals and books. We were called pages, which I found fitting. Today's workers have the much more mechanical title of stacks assistants. A motley crew of full-time supervisors and part-timers, mostly students from the university next-door, we pages sat in windowless sequestration on old wooden chairs around a scarred wooden table facing a rudimentary pneumatic-tube station. We were like a clan huddled around a fire, surrounded by a vast regimented forest of metal shelving standing at attention in the steely dark. Ranks that were cast in sudden light as we walked down the aisles, tripping sensors as we pushed small, wobbly-wheeled book trucks. We were on the hunt for volumes requested by the scholars above in the window-bright, graciously apportioned, hushed reading room, where our benign if exacting overseers, the reference librarians, helped researchers in their quests, gathered their scrawled call slips, coiled them into glass vials, spun the covers in place, and dropped them down a tube that inhaled them with a satisfying whoosh. The capsules hurtled through the dark then shot out onto the landing platform with a smack that jolted us fetchers into action. In between capsule arrivals, we read, talked, fidgeted, and slouched.

One of the cheerier of the full-timers could have time-traveled from the mid-nineteenth century. He had long, thin, blond hair that was always in motion, a regal nose, and print-dazzled blue eyes behind wire-rimmed glasses. He was a professor without a classroom, a free-range philosopher smitten with and buoyed by the ancient Romans and Greeks. He always had one of the small green or red, gossamer-paged volumes from the Loeb Classical Library in hand, committed as he was to carefully reading the entire series. He loved to share his joy in these time-tested texts, gesturing with his hands, shaking his head, lifting and dropping his shoulders, intent and utterly serious and yet also abashed and bemused at himself. I found his performances intimidating, captivating, refreshing, endearing, and inspiring. He was an apostle of rereading. He believed that a life in books and contemplation was a life to cherish. A gift of the gods. He cheered on my bookishness with profound camaraderie. With his ebullient approval, I read and reread the classic Greek tragedies. I ventured into Horace, Cicero, and the Stoics, with particular attention to Marcus Aurelius. I read Shakespeare freely and slowly. The continuum of stories and the quest for understanding felt cosmic in its vastness. Like starlight, these works delivered illumination from afar.

Another impressive coworker pierced my ears in the lavatory. Another, a small, seemingly shy occupant of his own world, turned out to have an unpleasant way of communicating that required a hunter's patience. I discovered this as I searched for a title in a remote quadrant of the dark stacks. As I walked down an aisle, scanning the call numbers, on an otherwise vacant shelf I saw a strange, decidedly unbooklike object. It looked like a living thing of some sort, possibly reptilian. As I slowed down with a frisson of fear, I saw it for what it was. That was shock enough, but that the human to which it was attached turned out to be the quiet, awkward page who couldn't make eye-contact was at once jolting and inevitable. I don't recall what subject area he chose to temporarily shelve his male member. And how long did he wait in the dark? What were the odds that a page would venture down that particular aisle? It was spooky down there; triggered by motion, the lights put you in the crosshairs of a predator. Was I the target, or was he waiting for any page working that day?

Most of us young women were already all-too versed in the aggression and inanities of men. I was mortified and shamed as the perpetrator scurried away. But as I shook off my initial alarm, I started to feel more worried about his well-being than mine. And I began to find it funny. What a ludicrous and risky expression of sexual frustration. What a mockery of the rigid order that ruled this fortress of categorization. His act made it a surrealist's library. His quiet offering and plea in that bastion of intellectual rigor, ruthlessly pragmatic experiments, and profitable conclusions was a bold if perverse protest. A reminder of human vulnerability. A silent "fuck you" to the academic-industrial-military complex. Or not. Maybe I was just trying not to feel victimized or too sorry for this deranged coworker. Compared to other unwanted and far more aggressive encounters and street harassment, this was nothing to freak out about. Thankfully, there were no repeat performances.

It was time to row forward, to leave Kansas City. Chicago would be my next port. I expected this Great Lake metropolis to be the first stop in a slow journey back to New York. I enrolled in the summer semester at art school so I could graduate early. We packed up what was left after our apartment was broken into and hit the road, me at the big wheel of a large rental truck with a terrified cat yowling piteously at my feet until the tranquilizers finally pulled him into sleep. I bounced and jostled along the interstate, full of hope, worry, and anticipation. A new city would inspire many changes and a whole new round of books.

Good Books, Books I Revere

Tell enthralling and haunting stories.

Present intriguing characters.

Illuminate the fantastic in the everyday.

Chart the currents, shoals, whirlpools, and tides
   of the mind.

Celebrate place down to the bedrock.

Trace life's infinite interconnectivity.

Celebrate all that is not human on Earth.

Take measure of what is it to be human.

Track ripple effects through generations.

Capture the textures of being.

Reveal nuance.

Explore the collective unconscious.

Weave a tight tale.

Embrace ambiguity.

Meander meaningfully.

Unravel cover-ups, lift veils, open curtains,
 raise blinds.

Raise hell.

Bring facts to vivid, significant life.

Venture into the wildly imaginative.

Explore psychological intricacy.

Explore moral dilemmas with gravitas.

Explore moral dilemmas with humor.

Tell the truth, the hard truth.

Find the humor, whenever possible, in difficult straits.

Honor and create beauty.

Honor and investigate pain.

Honor and nurture hope.

The Chicago River, Changing Direction

Stormy, husky, brawling,
City of the Big Shoulders

—Carl Sandburg, "Chicago"

This braggadocious poem by Carl Sandburg was all I knew of Chicago as a child. Years later I was struck by Sandburg's poem "Skyscraper." It depicts a tall building that "looms in the smoke and sun and has a soul." The poet describes how it fills with people from the country and the city and how "they mingle / among its twenty floors." I never imagined I would become one of those mingled people.

Every summer when we were kids, my mother's mother and stepfather fled their sweltering Bronx apartment and stayed with us in leafy Poughkeepsie. So, we were all together in front of the television

when the networks aired footage of Chicago police-
men viciously and methodically beating peaceful
antiwar demonstrators who looked just like the long-
haired college students little me swooned over in our
little river city. I was shocked and horrified. Chicago
seemed to be a foul and cruel town. But when I made
my way there years later to join art-school friends
who had found anchorage in the city, my perception
gradually changed.

As the initial excitement of arrival waned, I was
ambushed by the city's unrelenting flatness. I felt
depleted, as though lacking a key mineral or vitamin.
I felt exposed, treadmilled. Without the rise and fall
of land beneath my feet, without curving streets and
roads offering fresh views just around the bend, I felt
as though I was living on a colossal sheet of graph
paper. I felt small and enervated, trapped in an
endless grid of straight lines and right angles broken
only by the intimidating star intersections where
the city's great diagonal streets slanted through
the crosshairs of the vehicle-pounded verticals and
horizontals. Endless asphalt conveyor belts. I was

sensory-deprived, oppressed. And this was before the smack-down of winter. Nonetheless, I started to learn my way across the checkerboard of neighborhoods demarcated by ethnicity, race, and class, across the circuit board ranked with two- and three-flats and nose-to-tail parked cars. The straight-to-the-horizon streets ran like lines of text in a clamorous urban chronicle, each building percolating with hidden lives—just as words contain multiple shades of meaning.

I found that Chicago is a bricky town of harsh weather and bluster, hard work and avid play, pragmatism and creativity, violence and kindness, competition and comradeship. The neighborhoods were punctuated by humble churches and cave-like taverns, shoe-string family restaurants and noisy laundromats. Mercifully, the residential side streets were softened by arcing trees, their green leaves waving in the warm seasons, their branches etching the gray skies with intricate calligraphy in the spare cold times. The little yards and parkways were alive with sparrows, robins, cardinals, mourning doves, crows, squirrels, rabbits, rats, and stray cats. Here, too, were potholes, graffiti, broken glass, litter, and rubble. Incessant traffic, trains drumming and squealing, sirens, the roar of airplanes. The silence of abandoned cars, abandoned buildings, abandoned people. All were at stake on the immense game board.

This Great Lake city of many library branches has a three-branched river. For millennia, what are now called the North, South, and Main Branches were little more than sluggish streams moseying through marshlands. As Chicago writer and champion of the underdog Nelson Algren writes in his galvanic prose poem, *Chicago: City on the Make*, "To the east were the moving waters as far as the eye could follow. To the west a sea of grass as far as wind might reach." These humble river branches watered an ecotone, a place of transition and vitality, in this case, where the eastern forest morphed into the tall-grass prairie. For some twelve thousand years Native peoples, includ-ing the Ojibwe, Odawa, and Potawatomi Nations, as well as the Miami, Ho-Chunk, Menominee, Sac, Fox, Kickapoo, and Illinois Nations, thrived on the fertile earth nurtured by the three streams. Until white outsiders arrived, with the go-ahead of the federal government, and forced the people to leave their ancestral lands, violently seizing and radically trans-forming this exceptionally rich and valuable terrain.

Illinois joined the Union in 1818. Chicago incor-porated as a town in 1833 and as a city in 1837, and as the human population boomed, human waste was dumped into the Chicago River, especially the Main Branch, which delivered its vile cargo to Lake Michigan. On July 4, 1836, construction began on the first river canal. Then the boggy city raised its streets to build a sewer system that promptly increased the discharge of filth into the river and the Great Lake. A tunnel, ditches, a diversion channel, and an in-take crib were constructed. Then Chicago made history with a monumental feat of engineering and chutz-pah: this stubborn, might-is-right, dirty, brash, mon-ey-grubbing city managed to reverse the direction of its river.

When the Sanitary and Ship Canal opened in 1900, the befouled flow of the Main Stem and South

Branch defied the natural order of rivers and headed away from Lake Michigan, preserving it as a source of clean drinking water and protecting its aquatic ecosystem. But that bossy reversal meant that the toxic Chicago River was turned into a tributary of the Des Plaines and Illinois Rivers, which were poisoned in turn, thus killing off river life. Fourteen years later, construction began on the first sewage treatment plants and engineers continued to reshape the Chicago River to meet industrialized human needs. The North Branch was straightened. The North Shore Channel was built, with a dam at the confluence with the North Branch. To the south, the Cal-Sag Channel was constructed; the West Fork of the South Branch was filled in, and a stretch of the wandering South Branch was made to go straight, while the already chastened North Branch was paved, like Brush Creek. No curving allowed. No caressing the natural lay of the land. The rule of the man-drawn line prevailed. Could I live here?

Nelson Algren—to whom Eleanor Roosevelt presented the first National Book Award for *The Man with the Golden Arm*, an unflinching novel of poverty, drugs, and desperation—weighs in:

> The portage's single hotel was a barracks, its streets were pig-wallows, and all the long summer night the Pottawattomies mourned beside that river: down in the barracks the horse-dealers and horse-stealers were making a night of it again. Whiskey-and-vermilion hustlers, painting the night vermilion.
>
> In the Indian grass the Indians listened: they too had lived by night.
>
> And heard, in the uproar in the hotel, the first sounds of a city that was to live by night after the wilderness had passed. A city that was to roll boulevards down out of pig-wallows and roll its dark river uphill.

The "hustlers," to use Algren's term for the city's movers and shakers, were just as pragmatic about dispensing with human creations they viewed as impediments as they were about altering nature. As I marveled over the city's organically sculptural architecture, especially the lushly detailed, nature-inspired buildings of Louis Sullivan, I learned that these were survivors of a plague of reckless razing that obliterated structures of exceptional beauty and ingenuity. After Chicago's hastily assembled, wood-frame first edition burned to the ground, people quickly regrouped and built magnificent edifices of stone and steel, creations of vision and elegance known the world over, only to subsequently tear down many of these masterpieces to make way for parking decks and dreary office buildings. This wave of oxymoronic urban renewal was ordained by Mayor Richard J. Daley, the same mayor who ordered Chicago police to beat and tear gas peaceful antiwar demonstrators, onlookers, and passersby during the 1968 Democratic convention. As unique, uplifting public buildings and palatial mansions were desecrated and demolished, so, too, were thousands of cherished homes as vital Black neighborhoods were severed by thundering and polluting expressways and land was grabbed for the expanding Illinois Institute of Technology.

One building eradicated by the wrecking ball was the Mecca Flats, a massive, brick, Romanesque, four-story, U-shaped courtyard apartment complex. Built on more than two acres in Bronzeville at 34th and State Street on Chicago's storied South Side as a fancy hotel for visitors in town for the 1893 World Columbia Exposition, it was subsequently designated as a whites-only apartment building. After desegregation, it became a fabled home for hundreds of Black Chicagoans.

The dream and the struggle to own a home of one's own and put down roots shapes seminal works of Chicago literature, including the poetry of Gwendolyn Brooks, who came to the city with her family as a girl after they left Topeka, Kansas. Brooks became the first Black poet to win the Pulitzer Prize and the first Black woman to hold the position now known as the U.S. Poet Laureate. Brooks was Illinois poet laureate for 32 years, and an influential professor dedicated to inspiring young people and addressing social problems.

In Brooks' first collection, *A Street in Bronzeville*, published in 1945, "kitchenette building" explores the consequences of the diabolical practice of chopping apartments into even smaller spaces to squeeze in more tenants. These cramped quarters without private bathrooms occupied by entire, often extended families were the products of a particularly stifling form of racist containment and slum-landlording. Yet life percolates within these homes in all its rich contrariness as Brooks so astutely registers with barbed wit, seasoned compassion, and wry celebration.

Brooks got to know the Mecca Flats during the Great Depression when she took a job working for a tenant, E. N. French, who styled himself as an East Indian seer selling potions, cures, and love spells to his Mecca neighbors. "In the Mecca" is a many-versed, increasingly mythic ballad in which a woman searches for her missing daughter, knocking on the doors of her neighbors, each of which opens to reveal an entirely different world of human complexity.

The battle against systemic racism in the housing market is the catalyst for Lorraine Hansberry's watershed play, *A Raisin in the Sun*. Also set on the South Side of Chicago, the playwright's home ground, it tells the story of the Younger family: Mama; her daughter, college student Beneatha, who plans to become a doctor; Mama's son, Walter, an aspirational chauffeur; his wife, Ruth; and Travis, their 10-year-old son. Mama has lived in their currently rundown and overcrowded apartment since she married Big Walter. Now that he's died, she is waiting for the insurance money so that she can finally buy a house. She finds a modest home with a small yard where she can garden, a place she can afford and still have money left over to help Walter go into business and Beneatha attend medical school. But there's a catch: the house is in a white neighborhood. Soon an emissary from the Clybourne Park Improvement Association's New Neighbors Orientation Committee arrives at their apartment with an offer that's more of a threat: they want to pay the Youngers not to move where they won't be welcome.

When Chicagoan Hansberry, the youngest of four, was eight years old, her parents—her father was a real-estate broker, her mother a driving instructor—bought a house in an all-white neighborhood, precipitating legal battles as hostile neighbors sought to keep them out. The case made it all the way to the U.S. Supreme Court, where the *Hansberry v. Lee* decision in 1940 ruled that the restrictive covenant involved was contestable. Eight years later, *Shelley v. Kraemer* found such restrictions unconstitutional.

Longing for a home of one's own is also the seed for *The House on Mango Street*, by Sandra Cisneros, a poetic, episodic novel set in Chicago, the author's hometown. A narrative formed of exquisitely nuanced vignettes narrated by young Esperanza Cordero, it begins with a litany of her growing family's moves from one dilapidated apartment to another. Her parents tell their children that someday they will own a big house with a big yard. "And we'd have a basement and at least three washrooms so when we took a bath we wouldn't have to tell everybody." Finally, they acquire a house and move in. "But the house on Mango Street is not the way they told it at all. It's small and red with tight steps in front and windows so small you'd think they were holding their breath." Cisneros' tale of prejudice, economic struggles, family, community, coming of age, and being female is a poetic and heartbreaking microcosm of universal resonance.

As a newcomer to Chicago with friends to help me get started, I was fortunate. I felt less alien than in Kansas City, a sliver less "other." Being female can be a liability here as it is most everywhere, but at least I was less conspicuous as a Jew, a "Yankee," an "art girl." There was more diversity in Chicago in kind and spirit with all sorts of people tossed together in many parts of the city, especially downtown, the Loop. Chicago was more conventional than New York, but also less pressurized, less frenzied, its stoicism and brashness slotted down a notch or two. Rents were manageable; the scale of living navigable. Most significantly, there was Lake Michigan, the vast, cold, mutable inland sea tugged and spangled by sun and moon. I found an apartment in the Lakeview neighborhood and while there was no view of the lake from our block, one could walk to it and I did so often, finding respite and inspiration on the lakefront, an open space in which to breathe and recharge, take in the long view, feel awed and exalted, stirred, and girded for everyday struggles, disappointments, and flat-out weirdness.

My only plan for finding work was to follow the books. In a small green spiral notebook, I wrote "suggested job names":

reader—reads and prepares synopses for review by editor, etc.

archivist—pictures, photos in library

My vague notion was that I should work in publishing, which would combine my commitments to art and reading. These positions seemed to denote work I could do and might actually enjoy.

On another page I wrote "Publishers in Chicago." I found these in the *Literary Marketplace*, the pre-internet source of publisher information. My neat alphabetical list runs for seven little pages, naming mostly educational or academic publishers. I have no memories of contacting any of them. Most have vanished. The list is followed by three definitions for "Jacob's Ladder" and a list of French novels recommended by a brilliant high-school boyfriend turned friend. There's a page with lots of doodles around "Kroch's & Brentano's," then Chicago's premier downtown bookstore. The following page names my destiny: "Newberry Library." I wrote down the address, a phone number and extension, hours of operation, "non-circulating," the nearest subway stop, and, aslant in the top corner, my future boss's name—an addition after a phone call? My social security number is scrawled below that.

Like Linda Hall Library, the Newberry is a world-renowned private research institution established by a bequest from a well-off businessman. William Loomis Newberry prospered in banking, real estate, railroads, and shipping. He also served as the alderman for the city's Ninth Ward, and as president of the Chicago Board of Education (a public school is also named after him). Newberry stipulated that if his two daughters died without heirs, half his fortune would be put toward a "free public library." He died at sea on the way to France in 1868 at age 64. When his widow, Julia Butler Newberry, died in 1885 without any grandchildren, two trustees began to bring Newberry's hazy notion of a library to fruition. While water claimed the man, Chicago's Great Fire of 1871 took his book collection, which could have seeded the library. What, then, should the Newberry Library consist of? The Chicago Public Library was up and running, and another wealthy Chicagoan was building a library in his own name and to his own standards in another part of the city.

John L. Crerar amassed wealth and influence in the railroad industry and became an avid advocate for books, education, and educational organizations. A religious man, he also allotted a substantial portion of his estate to the founding of a free public library, but he had strict criteria, specifying that it "must not contain nastiness and immorality," such as "dirty French novels and all skeptical trash and works of questionable moral tone."

The John L. Crerar Library, established in conjunction with the University of Chicago in 1894, became a brother to Linda Hall in its dedication to medicine, science, and technology. This focus may have cued the Newberry trustees to distinguish their library by laying the foundation for a world-class humanities collection that ultimately encompassed Native American history, U.S. and Chicago history, maps and exploration, the history of the book, genealogy, the performing arts, and much more. The Newberry had two temporary locations in the neighborhood while the permanent library was constructed on what had been the Newberry homestead. The building was designed by architect Henry Ives Cobb and its first librarian, William Frederick Poole, who left his post as the inaugural librarian for the Chicago Public Library to head this new endeavor.

While Linda Hall gleams with mid-twentieth-century sleekness within its urban arboretum and neighboring college campus, the imposing granite Spanish Romanesque Newberry, built with stone fittingly sourced from its founder's birth state, Connecticut, and opened in 1893, commands an entire block on Chicago's Near North Side, standing across the street from the city's oldest park, Washington Square, which earned a memorable nickname as a plaque attests:

Washington Square Park 1842
Also known as
BUGHOUSE SQUARE
Chicago's Premier Free Speech Forum

The surrounding neighborhood fluctuated between wealth and poverty, and it was during a dramatic financial downturn that the adjacent mansions were turned into flophouses, slang for rooming houses, sheltering the working poor and the destitute. Bughouse, another catchy coinage, usually referred to a place for the mentally unstable. In this case it marked the park as an arena for the politically agitated and oratorically inclined, the soapboxers and the rabble-rousers. Unlike those who now rant and foment digitally under glass, often with their identities cloaked, these speakers put their bodies on the line.

When he was young, Studs Terkel, Chicago's legendary oral historian, writer of conscience, radio host, and raconteur-on-a-mission, lived within walking distance of Washington Square Park. In his autobiography, *Touch and Go*, Terkel recounts life at the Wells-Grand Hotel, a residence for men run by his father in the 1920s, where on "the glory nights at the lobby [there] were debates between the retired Wobblies and the good 'company men.'" Studs also relished the open-air debates at Bughouse Square, "In its heyday, during the 1920s and 1930s, there were five soapboxes on which the most celebrated speakers were allowed twenty minutes and then afforded the privilege of passing the hat." After profiling some of the more colorful soapboxers Terkel writes, "On the north side of Bughouse Square stands the Newberry Library. Miss Polly Fletcher was there at the library, third-floor reading room. She was of Dorothy Parker mien, and, seeing a student hanging around Bughouse Square, suggested some book or other for me to fool around with. Upton Sinclair's *The Jungle* of course. Ida Tarbell on the Rockefellers. Dreiser's *Sister Carrie*. Miss Fletcher definitely played a role in my political growing up."

Terkel played a big part in my Chicago education. I began with *Division Street*, Studs' first work of oral history published in 1968, in which he shares his conversations with seventy diverse Chicagoans. Terkel explained: "I was on the prowl for a cross-section of urban thought, using no one method or technique ... I guess I was seeking some balance in the wildlife of the city as Rachel Carson sought it in nature." I continued to read Terkel's groundbreaking works, books in which he widened his scope and deepened his inquiries into life's paradoxes and joys, from work to war, race, class, art, hope, and death. Having acquired early on the habit of listening intently to discussions of the issues of the day, he remained forever enthralled by the music of conversation and the transformation of memories into story. Having titled his last book *P.S.: Further Thoughts from a Lifetime of Listening*, Terkel taught us that listening is an art, that everyone's experiences are worthy of attention. He championed working men and women, artists and educators, activists and humanitarians. He was receptive and smart and interested in everything, and he knew how to get people to talk about what mattered most.

Terkel earned a law degree from the University of Chicago, but realized that he wasn't the lawyer type, so he turned to radio, working as a sportscaster, disc jockey, and actor, cast most often as a Chicago gangster. He switched briefly to television and hosted a talk show called *Studs' Place*. Outspoken in his liberal views, Terkel drew the ire of the Red Scare-era FBI and was blacklisted. Nonetheless, when Chicago's fine-arts radio station, WFMT, was formed in 1952, they recruited Terkel and so began a 45-year run as an on-air conversationalist extraordinaire. Terkel dazzled the writers, actors, and musicians he interviewed with his curiosity and knowledge, the avidity and acuity of his reading, his high attentiveness, and his unerring moral compass. Studs was a tireless defender of our freedom of speech and our freedom to read, speaking out against the banning of books and any and all interference with our intellectual freedom. He praised librarians as heroes.

Rick Kogan, the Chicago newspaperman, radio host, author, beloved chronicler of the city, and the son of two Chicago journalists, Herman Kogan and Marilew Cavanagh Kogan, who were close friends with Terkel, wrote in a *Chicago Tribune Magazine* profile, "On radio, Studs' brimming curiosity and 'feeling tone' carried him into the hearts of the world. Thousands of celebrated names shared their thoughts and feelings with Studs. But so did those who never made the headlines or gossip columns. Studs was always interested in the daydreams and truths of 'ordinary people.'" That's because, as Margaret Atwood discerns, Terkel is "an inheritor of the same strain of American idealistic romanticism" that inspired Walt Whitman, Mark Twain, John Dos Passos, and John Steinbeck.

Terkel was a hungry and insightful reader. Born Louis Terkel in 1912, he acquired his nickname because of his strong identification with the hero of James T. Farrell's novel, *Studs Lonigan*. He avidly shared his love for and faith in literature: the sheer, inexhaustible beauty of language; the power of ideas; and the ways art engenders compassion. Possessed of an extraordinarily sharp memory, Terkel could quote entire passages from John Steinbeck, Ernest Hemingway, Ralph Ellison, and many more. By discussing literature on the air, Terkel made talking about books part of the dialogue of everyday life. Sandra Cisneros writes, "It was Studs who introduced Pablo Neruda's poetry to my mother from the radio on top of the refrigerator next to the slouched loaf of Wonder Bread. The kitchen was my mother's classroom, and she was promoted from the ninth grade to the University of Life with a PhD. Studs schooled her. Studs showed her the way home."

I never imagined that I would meet people who were close to Studs and then Studs himself, talk books with Studs over drinks at literary gatherings, visit him at his home, go to dinner with him and other luminaries like E. L. Doctorow, and share a stage with him. I could never have predicted that I would have the honor of presenting the National Book Critics Circle Ivan Sandrof Lifetime Achievement Award to Studs in a New York University auditorium overflowing with literati whose standing ovations—one when an exhilarated 91-year-old Studs took the stage and another after I presented him with the award—pounded us in concussive waves. A bunch of us celebrated afterwards at the Algonquin Hotel where Dorothy Parker and her pals famously drank and quipped.

I am ever-grateful for receiving the Studs Terkel Humanities Services Award the year after his death at age ninety-six in 2008 on Halloween. I found out about Studs' passing right after my wallet was stolen while I was lunching with friends. The wait staff were wearing costumes and masks, adding to the disorienting, menacing, and mournful aura of the day.

***

When I was a kid, our new housing development had gravel roads. In early spring, when the snow melted and the cold, liberated water rolled down our sloping driveway, I would build Lilliputian levees and dams out of the small gray stones to create little rivers and lakes, moats and ponds. In Chicago, I used masking fluid to corral, direct, and layer water-based paint to create increasingly dense, detailed images. Book critics sometimes say that a writer's work is painterly to indicate a richly visual style. Perhaps I was pursuing a writerly form of painting. The mindscapes I created were in part inspired by my reading, which was leading me into the collective unconscious.

The first museum I was taken to as a young child was the Metropolitan Museum of Art in New York.

There I was indelibly marked by the Roman Egyptian mummy portraits of women, men, and children with large, gleaming dark eyes and somber expressions. How viscerally these ancient memorials affected me. I felt possessed, riveted. Why did I feel a sense of recognition? Why was it, I wondered, as I came of age, that the more art and literature one encountered, the more connected everything seemed? I often felt as though I'd found a portal into another dimension. I sought and cherished this sensation of deep accord, of profound commonality across space and time. When I came across the concept of archetypes, I knew it was the key. I turned to the works of Carl Jung, beginning with *Man and His Symbols*. There I found a wellspring of affirmation in his perception of the timeless and universal power of symbols, stories, and art. Jung distinguishes between the "personal unconsciousness" and a deeper inner realm:

> We also find in the unconscious qualities that are not individually acquired but are inherited, e. g., instincts ... In this "deeper" stratum we also find the ... archetypes ... The instincts and archetypes together form the

> "collective unconscious." I call it "collective"
> because, unlike the personal unconscious, it
> is not made up of individual and more or less
> unique contents but of those which are uni-
> versal and of regular occurrence … an omni-
> present, unchanging, and everywhere identi-
> cal *quality or substrate of the psyche per se.*

Jung diligently recorded his powerful and mysterious dreams and visions even as his rational, scientific self recoiled from their drama and riddles. He recounts how these experiences led him to walk away from his "academic career," and how lonely this solo inves-tigation was, how long it took him to understand the relationship between "inner; and outer." He dedicated himself to showing "that the contents of psychic experience are real, and real not only as my personal experiences, but as collective experiences which others also have."

Jung describes his study of mandalas and how it took him "virtually forty-five years to distill within the vessel of my scientific work the things I experi-enced and wrote down at that time" after he left the ideological framework Freud created and "had taken the step into darkness." Eventually he "hit upon this stream of lava, and the heat of its fires reshaped my life ... The years when I was pursuing my inner images were the most important in my life—in them everything essential was decided." Jung forged new and vastly influential interpretations of the human journey, drawing on treasures of human creativity and spirituality. Perhaps my faltering steps in the darkness would lead me to a "lifetime's work," however modest.

My notebooks, which come in various sizes and forms and are frustratingly erratic, contain many accounts of dreams. I came across a description of one dream I had while I was trying to figure out what I should be doing creatively and to support myself. "Dreamt I was a telescope, the kind that retracts and extends. I twisted and turned, getting longer & shorter —I could look through. Also, I was a like a snake shedding its skin, wriggling, writhing." In one of those moments of what Jung terms "synchronicity" that occur in a reading life, after I found the journal entry above, I opened my beat-up copy of Jung's indelible memoir once again and read this epigraph at the start of the editor's Introduction:

> He looked at his own Soul
> with a Telescope. What seemed
> all irregular, he saw and
> shewed to be beautiful
> Constellations; and he added
> to the Consciousness hidden
> worlds within worlds.
>
> —Samuel Taylor Coleridge, *Notebooks*

Jung steered me to Joseph Campbell, beginning with *The Hero with a Thousand Faces* and moving on to *The Masks of God: Creative Mythology*. The pleasure accrued by persisting through the complexities and not always felicitous writings of Jung and Campbell is found in the myths, folktales, and religious stories they gathered from all around the world. Here was the great singing web of our ancestors' struggles with the wild, love, family, longing, ambition, fate, death; the cosmic mysteries, and our tragic hubris and folly. These dense yet freewheeling books at once deepened and elevated my search. In my journals I wrote of my depression and discouragement, admitting that all I wanted to do was read and sleep. I was once again creating my own retreat in the midst of life's routines. I was sending myself to the underworld, withdrawing to a cave of dreams and myths, subsuming myself in the discoveries of others.

This immersion in foundational tales inspired me to read a book that had no role in my secular humanist childhood, the Bible. I needed to know these bedrock stories. If I could read massive novels, I reasoned, surely, I could read the Bible. And so I did, filling legal pads with notes; feeling awe, connection, recognition, and renewed outrage over hypocrisy, injustice, and bloodshed.

As I filled my mind with the ancients by night, by day at the Newberry I was part of a methodically organized and tightly run operation in a large corner room with many windows and half-a-dozen workstations. I had landed a trainee position as a finisher in the Newberry's pioneering conservation department and laboratory, established by leading book conservator Paul Banks. The conservators he trained there spread his preservation gospel and practices far and wide. In the bindery, skilled technicians took apart and stitched back together old books made of vellum and parchment. Books printed on acidic paper were dismantled, washed, and reassembled. We also bound periodicals.

My job was to stamp, with gold or silver foil, the book's title, author, and call number on newly constructed book covers and spines. I worked with cloth-covered boards, setting the type by hand. My station held a set of old wooden type cases with little rectangular cubbies for each tiny metal letter. I was spun back in time, minding my ps and qs, reading type backwards and upside-down. I set each letter in the composing stick, with the necessary spacing material and loaded the form into an old table-top hand press. I placed each cover carefully on the bed, and then set the thin, delicate foil—so easy to crimp or tear—gently on the cloth. It took all my strength and body weight to pull down the lever and stamp the foil into the cloth, to embed the gold and the silver into the embossed shapes the letters created as they bit into the threads. Over and over again I figured out how to best compose the text, over and over I plucked out the metal letters, the slugs. Again and again, I set the form, loaded it into the press, splayed the cardboard cover wrapped in durable plain cloth of blue, gray, green, red, brown, or black. Gently, gently I lifted the foil, every slight movement a gust of wind. I had to exert pressure but carefully so as not to shift anything. I needed a clean, crisp impression. I would remove the cover, carefully brush off the loose foil, inspect the embossed letters and numbers, set the cover down at the "finished" end of my worktable and take up the next order. I wore a white lab coat with my name embroidered in blue cursive about the chest pocket. I was slipping into a fugue state.

During my training, I brought in paperback books of my own to practice on, binding them with new covers. My favorite is the sage green cover for Ovid's *Metamorphoses*, the cover and spine stamped in gold with a beautiful serif font with a now forgotten name. I either chose it for its conspicuously large O's, or perhaps I used a different font to accentuate them. The book is an old cheap paperback edition of a translation by Rolfe Humphries published by Indiana University Press that I bought used, a book I marveled over, marking passages gently with pencil.

Spinning and weaving appear frequently in myths, folktales, fairy tales, and ancient sagas. Weaving can be a cosmic endeavor rife with danger, valor, and hubris. In the *Odyssey*, during the long absence of her husband, master weaver Penelope keeps the welter of opportunistic, avaricious, and aggressive suitors at bay by insisting that she will not remarry until she's finished weaving a funeral shroud for her father-in-law. For three years, she unravels each day's work each night. In *Metamorphoses*, I marked "The End of the Daughters of Minyas," the story about a king's daughters who stubbornly refuse to participate in the festivities celebrating Bacchus, the god of wine, ecstasy, and fertility. Instead, they stay inside at their looms, a commitment that offends the deity. Soon their palace comes under other-worldly attack and their weaving is transformed into emblems of Bacchus and his powers:

> And cymbals clashed, and all the air was full
> Of the smell of myrrh and saffron, and their weaving
> Turned green, and the hanging cloth resembled ivy
> Or grapevines, and the threads were tendrils clinging.
> Leaves burgeoned on the warp, and purple clusters
> Leaped from the tapestry's purple.

As darkness falls amidst all the clamor and fire, the sisters, "hiding in the smoky rooms" are slowly metamorphosed into bats. Did I feel then as I do now that this is a warning against always putting craft and art first?

Ovid also tells the story of Arachne, a young and skillful weaver who dares to declare that her talent for "spinning and weaving wool" is greater than that of Minerva, the Roman goddess of handicrafts, the arts, justice, law, wisdom, and victory. The goddess disguises herself as an old woman barely able to walk and tries to convince Arachne to "defer to a goddess" and to "ask her pardon." Arachne rudely insults and chastises the elderly woman and asks her why "your wonderful goddess" has refused her challenge to a competition. What ensues is one of the many reckless egotistical showdowns that propel myths, fairy tales, and folklore. "She is here," Minerva responds. But Arachne is unfazed: "Maintains defiance, with a stupid passion / Rushing to doom." The battle is on. Goddess and mortal weave at lightning speed. "Threads of gold / Were woven in, and each loom told a story." Ovid describes both creations in grand detail. At the end "Neither Minerva, no, nor even Envy / Could find a flaw in" Arachne's tapestry. Enraged, Minerva attacks her mortal rival, striking her on the head with her shuttle until Arachne hangs herself. "Minerva / At last was moved to pity, and raised her." The goddess lets Arachne live, but informs her that she will "hang forever." She then turns her rival into a spider.

Skirmishes and competitions were covert in the bindery. We started early and were admonished to be quiet. We were allotted only a half-hour for lunch, a too-brief break during which I often sat near a window, glumly watching that winter's incessant snow and reading as much as I could to keep my mind anchored and occupied rather than spiraling into a chilly gray inner void as inhospitable as the weather. I loved the library and was thrilled when I had a chance to visit its priceless collections, but those immersions were few and far-between. For the most part, I was on my feet all day doing piecework, hardly able to talk to my fellow technicians, each of whom was intriguing in their own way but skeptical of the young interloper more interested in reading books than conserving them. This could not last. This was not my future.

I started wondering if I was of a different subspecies than my fellow commuters while waiting on the El platforms during my first Chicago winter. I thought I knew what cold was; I grew up with snow and ice; I had a winter coat and boots and gloves. But I had never felt the assault of Great Lakes cold. We stood exposed to the icy blasts on wooden platforms dusted with snow and crunchy with salt thrown down to prevent the accumulation of ice and our slipping down onto the tracks. Most people around me were far from bundled up. Some were wearing jackets, many were bare-handedly reading their *Chicago Sun-Times*, their *Chicago Tribune*, neatly executing the efficient page foldings and turnings required to keep the paper from blowing about outside and then, once finally onboard the crammed cars, from impinging on other people's minute personal space. In the era of smartphone scrolling, newsprint origami is a lost art.

My fellow commuters were not hunched up, stamping their feet, blowing on their hands, or panicking as I was. I could not fathom their nonchalance. I was in agony. One particularly snowy, bitter morning, with no train in sight, I gave up. I hurried back down the slick stairs as best I could on frozen feet, limp-raced back to my apartment on unshoveled sidewalks, struggled with stiff, aching hands to get my keys out of my bag and into the lock, and leapt back into bed without taking off anything but my boots. I called in sick, burrowed under the covers, and wept.

I was barely getting by on my paltry trainee salary. I needed to make more money and I needed to feed my reading habit, even though my journal tells me that I was regularly checking out books at the public library, continuing my French literature immersion with such adventurous tomes as *Selected Letters of Madame de Sévigné*. I landed a second low-paying, book-anchored job working nights in a small, humble bookstore, the Book Market, located just north of the big triple intersection of Clark, Diversey, and Broadway on the North Side in a neighborhood busy with small restaurants, shops, bars, salons, low-key medical and law offices, and a shabby hotel. I remember it all with great precision; journal entries confirm it. But even with the help of a patient Chicago Public Library reference librarian, I can find no trace of that small enterprise. It was part of a local chain, and the ace librarian did find a *Chicago Tribune* ad from that time listing three other addresses for the Book Market, including one I remember on Cedar Avenue, and one far west on Diversey Avenue, but nothing on Clark Street.

In spite of this baffling lack of substantiating evidence, that now ghostly bookstore did exist, I swear. It offered a small, tired selection of popular and pulp fiction and lots of self-help. The books on hand that I was enthusiastic about rarely sold, leading to my initiation into the perverse bounty of "returns." Booksellers get reimbursed for unsold books, but instead of actually returning paperbacks, we ripped off the covers to send back for credit, tossing the desecrated books in the trash—except for the titles I brought home and devoured. We primarily sold newspapers and magazines, including a discouraging array of smutty publications relegated to the back corner beneath a large, curved mirror.

I was usually the sole night employee; the huddles of furtive boys and men clumped in the porn corner were annoying at best, potentially dangerous at worst. On the rare occasion when a guy actually purchased one of those tawdry treasures, the transaction was awkward, icky, aggressive or, in a moment of precious recognition, funny, yet still uncomfortable and debilitating. Each night at nine o'clock I had to shoo those miscreants out of the store. I locked up, turned off the lights, and retreated to the cramped, messy office in the back where I tallied receipts that never quite balanced, stuffed bills and coins into a zippered sack, and lugged it to the night deposit at a bank a few blocks away, hoping fervently not to be mugged. I then briskly walked the mile or so to my apartment.

This went on for a nearly a month and then, as though a romance novel in all its carefully formulated happily-ever-after improbability had come to life, Armando appeared, the new cop on the block. Back when pay phones still existed and sometimes even worked, cops actually did walk the beat, getting to know store clerks and waitresses, shooting the breeze, gathering and sharing neighborhood intel. Armando was tall, young, outrageously handsome and gallant. He would stop by toward closing time and stand next to the counter, broad shoulders squared, thumbs hooked in his holster. He would recount the evening's gossip and horrors while watching the pulp maulers who took their got-nothing-better-to-do time replacing the pawed magazines. Slouching and knee-popping, their body language spelling sarcasm and obscene assumptions, they slow-rolled their way out the door into the enfolding night.

Our little store was stocked by the Chas. Levy

Circulating Company whose trucks, jammed with
bales of newspapers, magazines, and paperbacks,
sported the motto: "Readers are leaders." The company's origin story is classic Americana. Young
Charles Levy (one source says he was fifteen, another
twenty), was living in poverty on the city's West Side
in 1893, a member of the struggling immigrant community of Eastern European Jews who fled antise-
mitic violence and headed further West than my relatives who made the shorter trek from Ellis Island to
New York City. Many Jews congregated in the Lower
East Side on the now emblematic Hester Street. In
Chicago it was Maxwell Street with its long-running
outdoor market where students and artists joined
other resourceful low-income folks in search of
deals. Levy's life took an abrupt turn toward success
when he entered a raffle and won a horse and wagon.
He put his prize to good use, delivering newspapers,
initially to blacksmiths' shops and ballparks. His
business grew rapidly; he brought his three brothers
onboard, and with the advent of motorized trucks
their distribution expanded in territory and content

to include magazines and paperback books. His son Charles, a Wharton student and a battalion commander who served with General George Patton in World War II, eventually took over. By the time I was slicing plastic bands off bundled copies of *Time* and Chicago's own *Playboy*, the Chas. Levy Co. was on its way to being the largest periodical distributor in the Midwest and among the largest in the U.S.

In the *Chicago Tribune* obituary for Charles "Chuck" Levy, who died at age 73 in 1986, Kenan Heise writes, "In 1956, Mayor Richard Daley`s Committee on Obscene and Pornographic Literature tried to get his firm to censor the books and periodicals it distributed. But Mr. Levy said that, while no publication his firm distributed had been declared illegal or immoral by any court or had been refused mailing privileges, his company could not function as a censor." Hence our inventory of skin magazines. I was then, as I am now, opposed to censorship and in full support of the freedom to read, yet I wasn't thrilled to be working in what verged on being an adult bookstore. I talked about this with the smart, hip bookstore manager, who was beset with personal woes, including her boyfriend's ever kinkier requests which she insisted on sharing with me. She decided to speak up and succeeded in convincing the bookstore owners that more porn rags were being mangled and stolen than purchased, so Levy stopped delivering them. She left it to me to order books to refresh the store's offerings, and soon mass-market titles were joined by literary classics and biographies and works in translation and short story collections and books of essays and poetry, and the store went out of business soon thereafter. And apparently took every trace of its existence with it.

River Styx

> Chicago. August. A brilliant day, hot, with a brutal staring sun pouring down rays that were like molten rain. A day on which the very outlines of the buildings shuddered as if in protest at the heat. Quivering lines sprang up from baked pavements and wriggled along the shining car tracks. The automobiles parked at the curbs were a dancing blaze, and the glass of the shop windows threw out a blinding radiance. Sharp particles of dust rose from the burning sidewalks, stinging the seared or dripping skins of wilting pedestrians. What small breeze there was seemed like the breath of a flame fanned by slow bellows.
>
> —Nella Larsen, *Passing*

Even though as a girl I loved my toy typewriter and enjoyed playing with an old behemoth of a manual Underwood relegated to the basement, as a depressed and unruly teen roaming the high-school hallways instead of sitting obediently in class, the clatter of the typing classroom unnerved me; it sounded like a factory. Not yet aware of Jack Kerouac's maniacally typed scroll or the fact that all the living writers I

admired typed and retyped their manuscripts, I imagined that creative writing was solely accomplished
in quiet and solitude with pen and paper. All I knew
about typists was that they were overworked and
underpaid women, banging out documents in typing
pools; belittled clerical workers in spite of how essential their demanding work actually was. I wanted no
part of that.

But, of course, I had to type for school and work,
and I did so ineptly. Now was the time to graduate from pecking to the real thing. My tight budget
allowed the purchase of a used manual typewriter
and an easel-style spiral-bound how-to-type exercise
book. I set both on an old Maxwell Street-acquired
kitchen table that wobbled on the uneven floor even
with paper wadded beneath its tired feet. I countered
the tedium of practice by setting an open, sweating
bottle of beer just out of reach of the typewriter's
platen. With each return, the typewriter shimmied
closer to disaster.

Our cat also proved diverting. A large, orange,
muscled, self-contained feline adopted from a shelter

after our beloved Kansas City cat died, he would leap neatly onto the unsteady table, sit behind the typewriter, and swat with great concentration at the rising and falling arms as though engaged in a cat-versus-machine boxing match. I tried to deter him, repeatedly picking him up and setting him on the floor, but he persisted. I gave into his stubbornness and kept typing the inane exercises, assuming that the keys hitting his paws would be annoying if not painful, or that he would get bored. Instead, he seemed to find it thoroughly engaging, even amusing. He ended up with little black letters stamped on his big, strong, tawny paws. When I stopped typing, he sailed off the table, landed lightly, and strolled over to a cozy spot to ponder, then lick off the jumbled messages of his temporary tattoos.

This gorgeous, composed creature never felt quite like ours, more like a boarder waiting for a break, and soon after the typewriter battle royales, he disappeared. I couldn't figure out how he exited the apartment, and I was worried sick and sad. We looked and looked and posted notices, and it all proved futile. Weeks later I was sure I spotted him sitting tall and regal in a window on the top floor of a three-flat far fancier than ours a few blocks away. I hoped it was him. I could accept his trading up as long as he was healthy and content. Wasn't I also seeking elevation?

***

"I've read a lot of books this summer like others watch TV—an Oxford University survey of English history and a survey of French history and innumerable encyclopedia entries and William Gass's *Omensetter's Luck*; Dylan Thomas's *Under Milk Wood* and *Portrait of the Artist as a Young Dog*; John Steinbeck's *Of Mice and Men*, and a whole slew of modern European plays." I listed them on the next page in my notebook, naming multiple plays by Brecht, Chekhov, Ibsen, Pirandello, Shaw, and Strindberg. I also read Eugene O'Neill and Robert Brustein's *The Theatre of Revolt*. I struggled through *Ivanhoe*; I suppose because it was frequently mentioned as an influence on British writers I admired.

I was much more in accord with *The Complete Works of Jane Bowles*.

I noted that I gave myself a gift, a handsome copy of Wallace Stevens' *The Collected Poems* because I was more "comfortable" with him than with many other poets. "I plan to read slowly thru the collection," I wrote. Underlinings and notes in that cherished book remind me that my favorites at the time were from *Ideas of Order* and *Parts of a World*. I marked up "A Fish-Scale Sunrise," a short poem of striking couplets, including, "And although my mind perceives the force behind the moment, / The mind is smaller than the eye."

Another journal entry reads: "I seclude myself like an invalid and read myself sick and then nap hotly on the sandpapery beach-warm couch to the drone of the fan. Too much effort to dress and walk through the threads of stares and cross streets according to colored lights and not drop a sandaled foot into shit, puke, or broken glass. I'd rather not squint in the deadening haze clinging to buildings and sky, muffling and wooly."

Like everyone I knew, I could not afford graduate school tuition, nor did I want to go into debt. So, I began looking for a job at a university that offered free tuition for employees. DePaul University's law library had an opening for a weekend circulation manager. I was pleased to discover that DePaul—alma mater to so many prominent Chicagoans, including both Mayor Daleys and library commissioner Mary Dempsey—had from its inception welcomed students from diverse backgrounds. This urban university offered full-time employees free tuition for many degree programs with the exception of the potentially most lucrative, business and law. DePaul would fund my MA in English in exchange for my helping law students succeed.

I had never worked in a tall building before, never had to regularly contend with crowded elevators, the vertical equivalent of crowded El trains. This solid 16-story structure, completed in 1916, was originally the Kimball Hall Building, designed and constructed for the W. W. Kimball Piano Company, founded by William Wallace Kimball (1828–1904) from Maine—the Kimball honored by the city's Kimball Avenue. At first, he only sold pianos, but after the Great Chicago Fire wiped out his inventory, he began manufacturing reed organs, then pianos, and his company became a resounding international success. Kimball received the World's Columbian Exposition Award at the historic 1893 fair. Chicago's lauded piano maker was buried in the city's historic Graceland Cemetery, along with Louis Sullivan and Mies van der Rohe, among many other luminaries. Kimball's handsome building at Jackson and State was eventually purchased by the Frank J. Lewis Foundation, which donated it to DePaul in 1955.

In Kimball's time, before electricity, before radio, before television, every aspiring household that could swing it had a piano. As Edward Rothstein wrote in the *New York Times*, "the piano was the instrument of a democracy, found in log cabins, parlors, brothels and the White House." The parlor piano brought music and entertainment into the home. People rushed out to buy the latest sheet music; that's how the hits were paraded. Published with elaborately designed covers, sheet music was a gold mine from the early 1800s on, with a particular surge after the Civil War during the "age of parlor music." The Smithsonian collection, Music for the Nation: American Sheet Music, covers the years 1870–1885 and contains 47,000 titles. Sometimes offered as a supplement to newspapers, sheet music continued to be printed in quantity for the public through the 1940s. Someone played; everyone sang. My grandmother was a talented pianist; she even had a band as a teenager in Philadelphia. But after she was betrayed and abandoned by her well-off first husband, my grandfather, she and her young daughter, my mother, were left traumatized in a small Bronx apartment with few comforts, let alone a piano.

Determined to redeem their difficult childhoods, my parents made sure their daughters had what they did not: parents who loved each other, a secure home, and music and dance lessons. They purchased a sturdy old upright piano at the Salvation Army, which my artist mother promptly "antiqued," covering its dark wood with swirls of ivory and gold paint, further degrading its tone. I was sent to a formidable teacher who wrote each week's assignments in black-and-white pebble-patterned composition books with brightly colored inks in large, bold cursive as assertive as her mighty bosom. One's progress was rewarded with small chalky white busts of classical composers. I loved learning to read music, another language, and using that keyboard came easily, though my commitment was low-key and fickle. I did not inherit my grandmother's musicality. I was drawn to all the arts and willing to try most anything, but eventually I realized that I had to concentrate on what came most naturally to me. While I reveled in and benefited from my forays into dance and music and my adventures in weaving, sculpture, photography, and painting, language was my element.

My position at the law library brought me into Chicago's clamorous downtown, the El-drawn Loop encompassing the Art Institute, Grant Park, Adler & Sullivan's Auditorium Building, palatial department stores (including Louis Sullivan's Carson, Pirie, & Scott Company Building, now the Sullivan Center), city hall, bars, restaurants, banks, and shops on streets dense with buses, taxis, and delivery trucks, and sidewalks thronged with hurrying workers and lingering trash pickers and panhandlers, cops and street preachers, pickpockets and harassers. People burbled up from the subways, poured down from the El, pushed into buses and elbowed their way out, jousting with umbrellas and hunching in the knifing wind, spinning litter, blowing grit, and diving pigeons.

I only had to thread my way through this gauntlet on three weekdays a week; as the weekend circulation manager I enjoyed the relative quiet of early Saturday mornings and Sunday afternoons and evenings. The weekend streets were less harrowing and more leisurely with shoppers, families, and tourists. There seemed to be more air; the soundscape was more of a hum than a ruckus. I was the first to arrive on the weekends, rising up in a blissfully empty elevator and unlocking the glass door. But then I would pause and steel myself because flipping on the lights was like shooting a starting pistol, precipitating a great scurrying, scampering, and whisking as the night shift, battalions of insects and mice, raced for cover and daytime rest. Once they were all safely out of sight and sound, I began preparing for the arrival of sleepy, reluctant student assistants and hungover and glum law students.

This was the most specialized library yet for me, the first in a university, the smallest, and the most intense and hectic. I had half of a tiny cubicle in the back-office area, but spent most of my time at command central, the circulation desk. The biggest draw was the materials professors put on reserve. The sudden post-class rushes to secure and photo-copy these pages felt like the swooping and fierce jockeying of pigeons when some wannabe saint cast bird seed or shredded bread upon the sidewalks, causing a flock to instantly materialize in a storm of wings, claws, and beaks. Law students pressed up against the counter and cawed out their requests, while others pecked, bobbed, preened, and paced impatiently behind them. Many of these determined future lawyers were from Chicago and its suburbs, but plenty were from farther afield, while the student assistants, mostly undergraduates, more reliably represented Chicago's rainbow of races and ethnicities. Some were fashion-plate beautiful, pressed and stylish and polite; others were T-shirt-casual, shrewd, and wisecracking. It was a place of ferment and concentration, friendship and rivalry, flirtation and complaints, hard work and irreverence.

The stacks were a study in uniformity with shelf after shelf filled with identical books in series that ran for decades and seemingly miles, each spine differentiated only by numbers and dates. There were walls of case books and case reporters federal, state, and regional; collections of decisions, opinions, opinions about opinions, and commentaries. Cases from city, county, state, regional, and federal jurisdictions and of district, circuit, appellate, and supreme courts were bound in weighty volumes. Acres were occupied by the U.S. Code, the U.S. Code Annotated, and the U.S. Code Service; by constitutions, legal digests, legal encyclopedias, legal dictionaries, statutes, and restatements of the law. The paper was thin, the type concentrated, the language impenetrable. Some relief was found in the slightly more welcoming legal treatises, hornbooks, and small paperback nutshells that offer overviews of specific areas like torts, bankruptcy, contracts, criminal law and procedure, property, taxation. We had stacks of the veritable key to the kingdom: *The Bluebook: A Uniform System of Citation*.

As cerebral as law studies are, some aspects of work at the library required brawn as well as brains. Many of the law books are large and heavy; reshelving them was weightlifting. As a federal depository, the library received government documents in surprisingly cumbersome shipments of microfiche (a word charmingly derived from the French for "little slips of paper")—four-by-six-inch pieces of film carrying microphotographs of thousands of pages. These thin, razor-edged cards had to be laboriously filed in a wall of microfiche drawers according to eye-crossingly complex codes of letters and numbers. These "little slips" were weirdly unwieldy. One day I was standing on a stool to reach the higher drawers. I pulled out a little shelf on which to set the full box only to have it tip over, the spilled microfiche forming a large, shiny fan on the floor in a sort of diabolical card trick, a slippery spread tricky and tiresome to dismantle.

Another taxing task was dealing with all the coins in the photocopy machines. Law students copied everything in those pre-internet days, and they had to pay for every page. I don't recall where they got their stashes of coins, but most of us routinely hoarded coins for payphones, the laundromat, vending machines, buses, and trains. Whatever the source, the copier coin boxes filled up fast. Staff had to empty them into money sacks, lift the heavy bags onto a metal cart and push them onto the elevator to reach a locked sorting and counting room. It was dirty, noisy, and boring work, funneling all those dimes, nickels, and quarters through the machines and accounting for every sum by hand on paper forms.

Fielding requests, complaints, tantrums, chitchat, laments, conundrums, and come-ons at the circulation desk veered from entertaining to funny, touching, exhausting, depressing, unnerving, and enraging. It was a circus of emotions and anxieties, egomania and insecurity, curiosity and competition. This was rarely a library of peaceful contemplation or escape from the pressures of life; this was an intellectual factory pounding out lessons and minting degrees; it was a boot camp, training future attorneys in conflict resolution, and their weapons were words, concepts, intellect, and attitude. The recruits were firebrands and paper-pushers, idealists and cutthroats.

Research is the foundation for the practice of law, and everything must be perfectly accurate, impeccably sourced and cited, and thoroughly supported. Complicated information had to be comprehended and memorized. The stacks were not caches of dreams and reflections, but rather vaults of rules and regulations. The poetic sense that the past is always with us was codified in precedents documented in tier after tier of casebooks; the past was foundation and framework. Here was rigor and tradition. Any bursts of improvisation, innovation, and creativity had to break through like determined plants growing from the crevices of stony desert cliffs.

I browsed these off-putting tomes and became intrigued by the knottiness, the repetition, the lexicon, the laboriously presented conditionality. Each page was a labyrinth. Why? I read Charles Dickens' *Bleak House* with sharpened appreciation. I understood the need for jargon as shorthand within the profession—every endeavor has its cant—but the law's gnarly language was an oppressive insider-outsider determinant.

Toiling by day among the monoliths of the law, at night I dwelled within the riverine realm of literature. Law and business classes were large and formal. Classes on the Romantic poets, Victorian novels, and literary criticism were small and intimate. We were a band of book-besotted night-searchers, not-for-profit seekers, dreamers in a sea of pragmatism.

Most of us worked full-time; many of us were returning to school after being ground down in the larger world. Some commuted from distant suburbs; others were city dwellers goaded forward by literary longings. Whether new to teaching or long-serving, our professors were passionate, thoughtful, respectful, and supportive. My guiding light was an impassioned virtuoso of the art of close reading, Bernie Brunner. I wrote in a journal: "Brunner is aggressive, abrasive, energetic, opinionated. We read Guy de Maupassant's "The Piece of String" word-by-word, leaving me overwhelmed." Our focus on traditional fiction, poetry, and essays was precisely what I longed for after my unconventional high school and art school experiences, but I often felt inadequate to the task. I did not have the solid, traditional academic foundation from which most English grad students launched their advanced studies. Instead, I had picked my way forward on stepping stones. A fumbling loner on a quest, I struggled to reach and enter the great hall of literary radiance. I wrote that attending classes was like "having to leap up and down to see fleetingly into a lighted window. Exhausting, unstable, inconsistent, awkward but seductive, exhilarating; one hopes to grow tall enough."

Since I was swerving from an undergraduate degree in fine art to a graduate English program, I had to take two prerequisite courses to prove I could handle the switch. One was a basic expository writing class, the first I'd ever taken, and I was discomfited by how little I really knew, technically, about the craft. The discussions about grammar and other formal concerns made me feel ignorant and disgusted with myself. I could write well enough for a casual practitioner, but I wrote strictly by ear. The other was a short story writing class. I was excited about that even though I was a total novice. Afterall, I reminded myself, it wasn't as though I'd ever felt confident in art school.

Our classes ran from six to nine at night. On those long days I kept myself stoked with cigarettes, coffee, and candy bars. We sat in unadorned classrooms on hard chairs; the teachers raised their voices as the El trains clattered by, and we were transported from that stone-clad Chicago skyscraper to Dickens's London, Wordsworth's Lake District, Dylan Thomas's Wales, Emily Brontë's moors, F. Scott Fitzgerald's West Egg, Flannery O'Connor's American South.

We would listen and talk and take notes; I would feel elated and buzzed and affirmed. After class, I would hurry to the El to catch what was then called the Ravenswood, a poetic name in sync with my literary preoccupation; it soon drearily became the Brown Line. The train cars, full of other night students, night-shifters, partiers, and couples on dates, clamored along twenty feet above the street, rocking so close to buildings you could see the faces of men slumped in the windows of SROs. It would all catch up to me then: the demands of work and school, the lack of nourishing food, the excess of caffeine, sugar, and nicotine, the excitement and the worries. I would have a book open; I wanted to read, I always want to read, but I would get woozier with each sway and curve, each abrupt halt and lurching start. At my stop, I would hurry down the stairs and walk briskly to my apartment. In spite of feeling dizzy, nauseous, and hungry, I was still elated by a night of literary revelations.

My courses included History of the English Language, Stylistics, Literary Criticism, English Renaissance Poetry, Modern British Poetry, 19th-Century British Novels—my ardor for *Middlemarch* is boundless—the Modern American Novel, American

Drama, and Comparative Literature, which turned out to be an immersion in modern German literature: Heinrich Böll, Alfred Döblin, Thomas Mann, Günter Grass. I remember this as a halcyon time. But in my journal, I expressed frustration with and rebelliousness against aspects of analysis that felt stale and pointless and rote. Mostly, I was aggravated with myself and my struggles to write clearly. I chide myself for being "clutter-brained." I write, "I'm learning to separate 'abstract,' 'arty' nonsense from actual prose. If I don't work hard at this, and long, I'm done for."

I read and reread Joan Didion. I was entranced by Marilynne Robinson's first book, *Housekeeping*, a poetic and haunting novel of two motherless sisters. I read Toni Morrison's *The Bluest Eye* and *Sula* in a state of awed suspension, of stretched awareness, and Alice Walker's *The Color Purple*. I read Nella Larsen in astonishment and more Saul Bellow. I looped back to read more Edith Wharton and Henry James. I read poets Elizabeth Bishop and Amy Clampitt and Philip Roth, Erica Jong, Maxine Hong Kingston, Grace Paley, Cynthia Ozick, and Paul Auster. I read Thomas

Wolfe, the stories and letters of Flannery O'Connor, and *Let Us Now Praise Famous Men*, which kicked off a James Agee obsession. I read Kenneth Patchen, Ken Kesey, Paul Bowles, Djuna Barnes, and Jane Jacobs, and now I'm free-associating as books flash by like silvery fish in the river shadows of memory.

Every experience was saturated, often fraught, at times ecstatic. I sought altered states. When I wasn't reading or writing, I was walking, daydreaming, dancing by myself in my kitchen instead of doing chores. Despite plunges into the cold waters of self-loathing, I was proud to be doing well in school while working a full-time job. I was looking ahead to the summer after I graduated. I wanted my obstinate sister to pry herself away from her life in Binghamton, New York, and visit me.

We only saw each other when I traveled to Poughkeepsie to see our parents. But now, she, too, seemed to be on an upswing, finally attending a college she liked, in a place she felt comfortable. She had a job she enjoyed well enough at an optometrist's shop, which seemed emblematic of her finally seeing a clear way forward, and a boyfriend who seemed more simpatico than her past loves: a much older, battered ranch hand; a handsome, young, and kind construction worker, guys our parents struggled to comprehend, but whom I knew fit into her grand passion for horses and ardor for motorcycles. I was ever the family go-between, the envoy, the diplomat, the soother, the reassurer. Not that I heard much from my sister; she was a reluctant correspondent. I insisted that she at least send me her poems. As a horse-struck girl—she went on to win ribbons for her equestrian skills—she had magic-ed up long, dramatic songs about horses and cowboys and heartbreak as we rode in the backseat on family outings, singing quietly, providing a melancholy soundtrack as we watched the voluptuous landscape roll by. As a teen, she took up poetry and that became our currency. Now that I'd earned my graduate degree, I wanted her to come to Chicago and help me celebrate.

She refused to fly; she hated cities. I offered to pay for two train tickets for her and her boyfriend, whom I had not met; I assured her that Chicago had plenty of open, green spaces. I told her she would love the lake. That I would take care of everything. I must have spoken to her on her birthday in early June. For my birthday in early July, she called me collect (oh, the drama of pay phones) from a noisy bar, clearly high and giddy over making me pay for my own birthday "gift." No one mocked me more than she. I laughed, glad to accept the charges, pleased that she remembered, relieved to hear her voice because however drunk and stoned she was, she did sound happy, taunting, and edgy, my beloved, elusive, thorny sister. I repeated my invitation. Give me a real gift, I said, come to Chicago. Come in early August. That first week, I can take time off. It will be fun, you'll see.

One month and a day later, during that first week in August, the phone rang in the early evening. It had been a hot sticky day. My mother asked me if I was sitting down. She sounded stern, deadly serious. What happened, I asked, feeling suddenly ice-cold, sinking reluctantly onto the bed, clutching our retro red dial phone I was so fond of, a vintage device so heavy I counted it as a weapon should the need arise. Now I clung to it like the edge of a cliff.

I could barely think about my sister's fiery, smoky death in her apartment. Of her boyfriend's death. They'd been at a party. They knew that they were too high to drive, so they left the car. But once home, either he or she passed out with a lit cigarette in hand. One can never be cautious enough.

Later I would think about my sister's fascination with Joan of Arc, of how she lit a candle for the immolated saint in the cathedral in Rouen. When she died, I was living among a cluster of small churches. Across the street at the end of our block a vertical sign on one of them declared: Pillar of Fire.

Later still, I realized that the day my sister died, August 6, was the day the U.S. dropped an atomic bomb on Hiroshima in 1945. This was the first use of a nuclear weapon on an actual city mere weeks after Trinity, the first nuclear explosion, was detonated in New Mexico, on July 16, 1945. On August 9, they, we, dropped the second bomb on Nagasaki. These world-changing attacks were instigated by a team of scientists led by Enrico Fermi in an improvised laboratory beneath Stagg Field on the University of Chicago campus.

A half-life is the time it takes for something to be reduced to half its previous power, to become unstable. In the nuclear context, a half-life is the amount of time it takes for radioactivity to decay to half its potency, for a radioisotope to diminish in strength. Some forms decay quickly, in hours, even minutes. But other isotopes have half-lives calculated in tens of years, in thousands. Plutonium-239 has a half-life of 24,000 years, during which it remains deadly. Radioactive waste ticks beneath the sea, in our soil, inside canisters in cooling pools, interred in tunnels and caves, and sequestered in concrete casks, vaults of poison standing beneath sun, stars, and moon.

To lose one's only sibling is to lose half of one's life. To be reduced to half of oneself, to be bereft of shared memories and understandings, of a unique, guiding intimacy. To be left with a book half-burned.

I went to Poughkeepsie right away. I was worried sick about my parents. Relatives arrived from all over;

close friends mobilized. Everyone wanted to know what to do, how to help, where to donate. We did not belong to a temple, but the rabbi for the small city's largest congregation and his wife were neighbors and friends, so the good rabbi conducted the funeral, and a plot was made available in the Jewish cemetery. My parents were admired, adored, and loved for being so very warm, generous, smart, attractive, classy, and fun. Beyond their large circle of friends, they were known by many for all their community volunteer work and support of local artists. My mother's paintings were prized, and she donated many to fundraisers for worthy organizations.

I remember a vast crowd at the service. The funerary car procession was miles long, or so it seemed. We were in a limo, and I had to keep taking off my glasses; the lenses kept getting encrusted with salt from my tears. I showed them to my mother in wonder, and with a strange solemnity she looked closely and said, "I've never seen that before, never thought of it." We were like curious children. We were in profound shock.

The rabbi said kind and thoughtful things about our family that I only remember as a sort of gentle murmuring, but I snapped out of the fugue of grief when he began to read, with genuine feeling and insight, the tenth section of William Wordsworth's "Ode: Intimations of Immortality":

> What though the radiance which was once so bright
> Be now for ever taken from my sight,
> Though nothing can bring back the hour
> Of splendour in the grass, of glory in the flower;
> We will grieve not, rather find
> Strength in what remains behind;
> In the primal sympathy
> Which having been must ever be;
> In the soothing thoughts that spring
> Out of human suffering;
> In the faith that looks through death,
> In years that bring the philosophic mind.

I was stunned. The kind, wise rabbi looked outside the parameters of religion to art in generous acknowledgment of our way of being in the world as a family of readers with a poet among us, now lost so young. He blessed us with that beautiful proven poem of loss and renewal. I knew then that I was choosing to dwell in a realm that would always sustain me. I saw that literature was a river, enduring and deep, that it flowed without ceasing across space and through time. I knew that I could rely on it, that I could always immerse myself in it and find sustenance and hope.

People were kind and sympathetic when I returned to Chicago, bruised, sorrowful, staggered. I have wisps of book memories from that stunned time. I dove into Sylvia Plath, the poems, the fiction. Was this because she died young, too? Because she struggled with demons and fury? My sister, an all-but secret poet studying psychology and kabbalah, was not suicidal, but she raced along the edge; she courted the rush of risk; she had a streak of self-destructiveness. I was much the same, though more covertly, and somehow, I was able to stay anchored. I was profoundly fortunate. I had a few rules. One, it hurts to say, was to not smoke in the house.

I dreamt of fire in the wake of my sister's death, and to this day I panic when I smell smoke. But more often I dreamt of water, fire's antidote. I dreamt that my sister and I could live beneath the waves. I dreamt that I was trying to rescue her from drowning, that I was drowning. I dreamt of tidal waves and vast rivers and being lost at sea.

I carefully noted the date I acquired my copy of *Johnny Panic and the Bible of Dreams*, just twelve painful days after my sister's hellish death. Plath, like most poets, struggled with the puzzle of how to make a living as a writer. She hoped that she could produce the sort of well-paid, entertaining short stories published in glossy magazines in the mid-twentieth century. But Plath couldn't suppress her intensity, her lacerating observations, her simmering anger. In the introduction to this early edition of her fiction, Plath's husband, the English poet Ted Hughes, not yet identified as the enemy, wrote that Plath worked "in the records office for mental patients in the Massachusetts General Hospital in Boston," a job that gave rise to the irresistibly titled title story, dated December 1958. It begins:

> Every day from nine to five I sit at my desk
> facing the door of the office and type up

other people's dreams. Not just dreams. That wouldn't be practical enough for my bosses. I type up also people's daytime complaints: trouble with mother, trouble with father, trouble with the bottle, the bed, the headache that bangs home and blacks out the sweet world for no known reasons. Nobody comes to our office unless they have troubles ...

Maybe a mouse gets to thinking pretty early on how the whole world is run by these enormous feet. Well, from where I sit, I figure the world is run by one thing and this one thing only. Panic with a dog-face, devil-face, hag-face, whore-face, panic in capital letters with no face at all—it's the same Johnny Panic, awake or asleep.

... what I mainly do is type up records. On my own hook though, and completely under cover, I am pursuing a vocation that that would set these doctors on their ears. In the privacy of my one-room apartment I call myself secretary to none other than Johnny Panic himself.

Plath died by fire, using her gas stove to end her life. I read and reread Virginia Woolf, who wrote of the sea, of water and waves; she also died by suicide, giving herself over to the River Ouse, stones in her pockets.

"Such are the visions which proffer great cornuco-
pias full of fruit to the solitary traveler, or murmur
in his ear like sirens lolloping away on the green sea
waves or are dashed in his face like bunches of roses,
or rise to the surface like pale faces which fisher-
men flounder through floods to embrace," so Woolf
intones in *Mrs. Dalloway*.

Our perceptions of oceans, rivers, lakes, ponds,
brooks, and puddles, of rain, sleet, snow, and ice
coalesce in an organ made of water. Seventy-five
percent of our brain consists of this crucial element;
our heart contains even more. Water is life and a universal symbol of transformation, rebirth, and cleans-
ing. Of depth and contemplation. I went to the shore
of Lake Michigan often, seeking solace in its silent,
secretive stillness; its cresting waves, shimmering
dimples, and shadowy ripples; its mirroring of the
clear sky, of intricate clouds feathery or majestic.

I first read Caribbean-born Jean Rhys during
this acute time of mourning, a daring fiction writer
who lived on the knife's edge and, propelled by
rage, exposed with radical incisiveness the confines

within which women struggled. I read more William Gass, Ann Beattie, John Cheever, James Purdy, back to Dostoevsky and Tolstoy and Nabokov. Wallace Stevens was ever a light in the gloom, as in "The Idea of Order at Key West":

> The sea was not a mask. No more was she.
> The song and water were not medleyed sound
> Even if what she sang was what she heard,
> Since what she sang was uttered word by word.
> It may be that in all her phrases stirred
> The grinding water and the gasping wind;
> But it was she and not the sea we heard.

These expressions of passionate attention to life and language, of pressing questions, hard-earned insights, conscience, compassion, and audacious artistry granted succor and sanctuary. They were vessels and anchors, sun and stars, maps and charts. I trusted the river of books, that perpetually flowing and vital current with its deep channels and bright shoals, its shores of sand and rock, trees and grasses, its canyons and valleys, its many creatures.

***

Battered by grief, I needed a fresh start, a new place, more compelling and challenging work. Once again, I researched Chicago publishers and read job listings. I learned about the American Library Association and its publishing department. A not-for-profit organization supporting librarians and libraries struck me as a possible harbor for my bereft bookloving self. Hired as an editorial assistant in the book department, I felt as if I'd found my habitat. Not only was my reading habit valued, so was my impulse to write about what I was reading. Every tributary converged as I was encouraged by perceptive colleagues to write freelance reviews for ALA's book review magazine, *Booklist*. Then, in a surge of life-defining good fortune, I was able to join the staff as an assistant editor. I was docked in a busy port, where books arrived daily from publishers and were then sent out to reviewers in a perpetual flow. Captivated by this literary cargo and by the cyclic process of putting a magazine together, which requires both visual and language skills, I was wholly occupied, my calling anchored, structured, and confirmed. Here I could read and write and support myself within a community of kindred spirits. Dear Reader, I found my place in the world.

Why Read?

To be transported.

To be transfixed.

To be spun.

To be stunned.

To be shaken.

To be rendered.

To be mended.

To be disarmed.

To be armed.

To be torn asunder.

To be made whole.

To be anchored.

To sail free.

To learn.

To unlearn.

To take refuge.

To embark on a quest.

To feel less alone.

To cherish solitude.

To remember.

To forget.

To swim in words.

To disappear.

To affirm.

To question.

To find.

To lose.

To grow.

To clarify.

To seek enlightenment.

River without End

The river
where you set
your foot just now
is gone—
those waters
giving way to this,
now this.

—Heraclitus

Bookish as I've always been, I didn't much like school. I found my own course of reading assignments much more exciting. How fortunate I was to be able to read voraciously from a very young age. Reading is thriving. It's a bedrock ability. I can hardly grasp the fact that we fail to teach this essential skill to so many children. Two-thirds of American students are not able to read at their grade level. This is unjust, undermining, and mystifying. The literacy rate in the United States is around seventy-nine percent, with fifty-four percent of adults reading below a sixth-grader's literacy level. People who aren't taught to read well are at a cruel disadvantage. They struggle to secure well-paying jobs. They're unable to access information that would help them cope with all the challenges they face. They're denied the bliss and respite of disappearing into a good book. Far too many of us are just getting by in so many ways; not being able to read makes life exponentially more grueling, dangerous, lonely, discouraging, confounding, and muffled. Because reading is a path to freedom, throughout history enslavers and fascists have found ways diabolical and brutal to silence book people: humanitarians, educators, writers, journalists, publishers, librarians, and booksellers.

As I revisited books and journals and looked back to my life of free-range reading, wading knee-deep in the river, we were hit with a precipitous surge in book challenges and book bans across the country. This ongoing assault against our freedom to read disrespects and denies the expertise of librarians and teachers; disrupts, sabotages, and threatens libraries and schools; and endangers people's privacy and safety, their very lives. Politically orchestrated efforts to "protect" children and teens from books that a few adults find problematic or books they were told were dangerous by political organizations, deny young people a crucial rite of passage: discovering books that assure us that we are not alone in our quandaries, longings, fears, and dreams. We grow and learn when we read books that explore the diversity and complexity of life, that inspire us to think and question, create and contribute.

The freedom to choose what to read, along with countless other life choices, is intrinsic to democracy. Most books censored as inappropriate are written by or are about the many people who were denied their rights, who were left out of the mainstream American mythos of the rugged individual: women, people of color, the LGBTQ + community, immigrants, and activists. Objections have been raised about books that chronicle the hard truths about American history, foundational facts we must face if we are ever to achieve a more equitable and just society.

Political and cultural conflicts are surging in conjunction with the worsening climate crisis. Battles against reading and the teaching and valuing of history and science are the exact opposite of what we need to navigate a volatile world. Being informed can be a matter of life or extinction. Book bans imperil our future.

Mine is but one story of one child who found her way forward with books, who was fortunate to have adults support her need to read. Countless young people survive trauma, despair, anxiety, loneliness, deprivation, confusion, bullying, self-loathing, and boredom by reading, by finding refuge in a well-stocked library, by finding mentors who encourage their quest. People of all backgrounds in all walks of life can attest to this same rescue, this same river-of-books voyage to selfhood. A love of books ensures that one always has something to look forward to. Life is effortful, often draining; reading replenishes and revitalizes. Reading provides a context for one's feelings and experiences and hones one's sense of meaning and purpose, right and wrong.

My work gives me a bird's-eye view of the book world and I can attest that, finally, there are more books by more diverse writers on more subjects. There have never been more forms of books or more ways to borrow or acquire or recommend and share books. There have never been more avenues for constructive responses to books. This abundance also means that there have never been more opportunities to malign and censor books, to threaten writers and those whose professions involve sharing books, especially with young readers. Like a river that bends back, that is diverted, dammed, or runs dry, the long pursuit of truth and justice does not flow steadily forward. It spirals back, sometimes way back, then slowly winds forward once again. The waters can be murky and toxic. In times of reversal, blockage, misdirection, and defilement, we need to champion reading and writing, journalism and scholarship, books and libraries. We the readers far outnumber the book-banners, the deceivers, and the deniers. In any way we can, however quietly or conspicuously, we must reject orchestrated fear and hate, propaganda and grievance, manipulation and corruption. Everything counts, and everything is connected.

Given all the book lists I made as a young reader, a magazine titled *Booklist* seemed like my destiny. There are few publications like *Booklist*, and I was wildly lucky to find a job there. Whenever things turn grim, as they inevitably do, I remind myself to be grateful for having work that keeps me supplied with books and that requires me to read. I have boundless admiration for all the adults outside the book world who make time to choose, find, and read books while conducting lives bristling with myriad demands. All of us insiders are deeply reliant on and in debt to readers, to booklovers who recommend books, join book clubs, attend author events, give books as gifts. Readers, I bow to you.

Every book is a risky undertaking; books demand attention, receptivity, empathy, and time as well as skepticism, patience, and analysis. Serious reading requires a willingness to be moved, to confront pain and fury, to question oneself and one's world. I weep while reading books about crimes against humanity and nature. I rage in the grip of books about greed, lies, and corruption. I am grateful to writers who devote themselves to such wrenching subjects, who spend years of their lives searching for the hidden truths about atrocities, pushing through their own sorrow and anger to document and analyze malfeasance and horror, realities we need to face in order to understand who we are as a species as we so precipitously and ineptly dominate life on earth.

I object to pulled punches, sugarcoating, whitewashing, greenwashing, pandering, and blandness. I seek razor-sharp, deep-digging, intellectually exacting, psychologically astute, and beautifully written books. I want books that make me laugh, that make me swoon, that rekindle awe. Books resplendent in style and substance. I hope that each book is another piece of the puzzle, snapping into place. We should read adventurously. The more varied our reading, the more detailed, intricate, and vital our perceptions become. I have the good fortune to be able to readily read new writers, to push myself to read about subjects new to me and new takes on enduring interests. Reading intrepidly is a form of lifelong learning, continuous continuing education. Reading is a ceaseless round of connecting-the-dots and filling-in-the-blanks. An ongoing refinement of navigational charts, soundings of the depths, and one's internal map of the cosmos.

Narrative nonfiction keeps us richly informed and enmeshed in the web of life as writers translate the gleanings of research into true stories, evoking emotions and exploring the consequences and resonance of events, personal experiences, scholarly findings, and creative quests. The very existence of powerfully conceived and lucidly written nonfiction generates hope as evidence of our better nature, our willingness to learn and change.

Biographies enrich our grasp of humanness, of history, society, and culture. The in-depth chronicling of one person's life illuminates the lives of many others. The tireless sleuthing, interviewing, reading, analyzing, and writing biographers undertake is a mighty effort, a demanding commitment. To spend years of your life studying and recounting the life of another is a complicated and fascinating form of channeling and communion.

Essays are heady and bravura performances that expose the mind at work in a concentrated quest for understanding. A question or a riddle fires a writer's imagination, inspiring inquiry and reflection. The result can be an argument, a confession, a critique, a manifesto, a balancing act. Essays are inspiriting, provoking, and brain-tuning.

I never cease to marvel at the many dimensions, nuances, and investigations built into fiction, novels and stories that capture the churn of our emotional lives, the force of memories, the gravity of obsessions, the web of lives. The most resounding fiction nests inner intensity within astutely rendered locations, social contexts, complicated relationships, and bewildering predicaments intimate and communal. The creation of vital characters and places out of mere words does feel like magic. Stories that offer original, deeply considered views of human traditions and innovations, suffering and survival, love and epiphanies are endlessly engrossing. Fiction writers observe, interpret, imagine, and experiment, writing on multiple levels as they translate experiences sensuous, emotional, and intellectual into magnetizing prose. Page by page, they select meaningful details, track time, orchestrate conflicts, minutely trace human interactions, invent dialogue, and summon the beauty and terrors of the natural world. The complexity, command, and insights of fiction cohere into an enchantment of measureless meaning and resonance.

Most mystical of all is poetry. Poems reach far into the terra incognito of the psyche and the collective unconscious. Poetry heightens our awareness of the tricky dynamics and perverse contradictions of thoughts and feelings, the weight and beat of words, the look and sound of letters and lines, the music of language and silence. Poetry's distillation, subtleties, patterns, imaginative leaps, candor, metaphysical visions, and creative whirls startle us into new recognitions.

Just as an ecosystem needs a diversity of species to thrive, just as human communities need human diversity to remain vital, just as healthy eating requires an array of nourishing foods, vibrant and sustaining reading requires multifariousness. I've found that cultivating receptivity to diverse voices, stories, points of view, and analysis fosters a richer life. As a constant reader, I feel equipped to face loss and adversity; I feel grounded in different modes of being. I feel buoyed and ballasted.

***

My parents, Bronx high-school sweethearts, were ardent readers. My father, who dropped out at age fifteen to work when his family became unhoused and split up to stay with relatives, schooled himself in libraries and on the job. He became an electrical engineer, working first in aviation and then for IBM. Having a stable home and family meant everything to him. Not only did he work hard to support us, even when he longed for a less regimented career, he also made sure we had fun. My father loved to read biographies and books about history, cosmology, technology, and baseball. He kept reading even as his eyesight deteriorated, switching to a tablet to boost up the font size.

My artist mother was able to graduate from high school. She kept a spotless and welcoming home, cooked and baked with elan, and took community college classes. She had many friends. She loved to talk, shop, party, and travel. She was a tireless organizer and volunteer. And she managed to create many exquisite works of art, getting up hours before the rest of us to work before household demands intruded. She was also a steadfast reader; she and I shared a passion for literary novels. But long-suppressed anguish finally conquered this willful dynamo. Much to our bewilderment, my beautiful mother did what her maternal grandmother had done: she took to her bed. I remember my mother using that Victorian phrase when I was a girl and she talked about how Fanny was overcome by grief after losing her twin sons in the influenza epidemic and her husband to a fatal fall in their home. A fate my mother barely avoided when she plunged down the staircase in our house, sustaining injuries that were never properly repaired and that eventually caused her to lose mobility and suffer constant pain.

Books saved my mother during her difficult last years. As her life contracted, my mother turned to mysteries for distraction, until she told me she'd had enough of death, no matter how cozy the tale. Beguiled and comforted by the Hallmark Channel, much to our bafflement—all those Christmas movies!—she decided that she wanted to read romance novels. I was happy to keep my mother supplied with fairy tales about true love prevailing over adversity, about strong, independent, even irascible women taking charge and showing men how to become better humans. Some of those romances were funny, others dark; some were sweet, others sexy, and all were delectably suspenseful because this genre, this book medicine, promises a happy ending no matter how drastic the obstacles to love become. I bought these reliably reassuring paperbacks by the armful; we gave them away by the bagful, and I bought more. My mother read romances for hours during the day; a lifelong insomniac, she read for much of the night. She looked young and rosy as she sighed over these tales of triumphant passion. Reading love stories kept the love she felt for my father radiant as he struggled with the distancing ravages of age.

My bedbound mother read romances while my father was hospitalized, while he went to numerous doctor appointments after returning home, when he had to go back to the hospital to undergo heart-valve surgery, as he recovered in a rehab facility, and when he came home again. My wise, funny, caring, problem-solving father kept as active as he could manage, but his body could not keep up with his sharp mind. Finally, he was rushed back to the hospital. This time he would not return. In spite having taken to her bed, in spite of her disability and pain, my mother was basically strong and healthy. But somehow, she made sure that she and the love of her life fulfilled the romance genre's guarantee of a happy ending. She died quietly at home before I even told her that her husband was gone. Not even death could sever their bond.

Books kept me from capsizing during my parents' declines, abrupt and mysterious near-simultaneous deaths, and the onset of shock and mourning. And books continue to carry me through the many waves and eddies of grief.

In writing this reading chronicle, I had to resist the powerful magnetic pull of my usual reading regimen and my preference to lose myself in someone else's book. Reading for *Booklist*, reading on deadline, is ever-urgent, yet rare is the day that I can read during official work hours. So, I read in the evening and into the night. I read on weekends and holidays. I read in cars, trains, and planes, waiting rooms and lobbies. I read attentively and inquisitively, pen-in-hand, pausing often to look things up, then getting distracted as these searches lead to yet more reading. The rereading I did for this book was exhilarating and validating. I went a bit rogue and gathered more quotes and wrote more than I was able to fit between these covers. There is so very much to read and think about.

As I write this, libraries are restocking their "New Arrival" shelves and bookstores are reorganizing their front tables. Readers are adding titles to their to-be-read lists, buying and checking out books, giving books to others, stacking books by beds and easy chairs, and stocking their devices with e-books. Writers in the spotlight are being interviewed and everywhere writers are filling notebooks and laptops. Little ones are sounding out words as a bigger person shares an open book. Reading is intimate and communal, enlightening and sustaining. Season by season, through storms and drought, reading helps us navigate the river of life. Dear Reader, read on.

The Books

Never the Same River, Never the Same Book

Heraclitus: Fragments. Translated by Brooks Haxton.

The Hudson River, the Source

A Reader on Reading. By Alberto Manguel.

When I Was a Child I Read Books. By Marilynne Robinson.

Chinese Fairy Tales. Translated by Marie Ponsot. Illustrations by Serge Rizzato.

Just So Stories. By Rudyard Kipling. Illustrated by H. B. Vestal.

Winnie-the-Pooh series. By A. A. Milne.

Grimm's Fairy Tales. By Jacob and Wilhelm Grimm.

Writers on the Air: Conversations about Books. By Donna Seaman.

What to Read and Why. By Francine Prose.

A Natural History of the Senses. By Diane Ackerman.

Little Women. By Louisa May Alcott.

Bone Black: Memories of Girlhood. By bell hooks.

Meg, Jo, Beth, Amy: The Story of Little Women and Why It Still Matters. By Anne Boyd Rioux.

Recitatif. By Toni Morrison.

On Girlhood: 15 Stories from the Well-Read Black Girl Library. By Glory Edim.

Hiroshima. By John Hersey.

The Fate of the Earth. By Jonathan Schell.

Ceremony. By Leslie Marmon Silko.

Underworld. By Don DeLillo.

Oh Pure and Radiant Heart. By Lydia Millet.

David Copperfield. By Charles Dickens.

Calm Sea and Prosperous Voyage. By Bette Howland.

The Catcher in the Rye. By J. D. Salinger.

Great Neck. By Jay Cantor.

Reading High

An Unspoken Hunger: Stories from the Field. By Terry Tempest Williams.

The Diary of Anne Frank. By Anne Frank.

Mary Jane. By Dorothy Sterling.

Close to My Heart. By Dorothy Sterling.

Lord Jim. By Joseph Conrad.

A Room of One's Own. By Virginia Woolf.

The Sea around Us. By Rachel Carson.

Slaughterhouse-Five. By Kurt Vonnegut.

Demian; *The Glass Bead Game*; *Steppenwolf*. By Hermann Hesse.

Soul on Ice. By Eldridge Cleaver.

Cry, the Beloved Country. By Alan Paton.

Another Country. By James Baldwin.

The Armies of the Night. By Norman Mailer

Slouching Towards Bethlehem. By Joan Didion.

Lady Chatterley's Lover. By D. H. Lawrence.

Journey to Ixtlan. By Carlos Castaneda.

Custer Died for Your Sins: An Indian Manifesto. By Vine Deloria Jr.

Virginia Woolf: A Biography. By Quentin Bell.

The Idiot. By Fyodor Dostoevsky.

Nature Writing: The Tradition in English. Edited by Robert Finch and John Elder.

Walden and Civil Disobedience. By Henry David Thoreau.

The Outermost House. By Henry Beston.

Desert Solitaire: A Season in the Wilderness. By Edward
    Abbey.

Pilgrim at Tinker Creek. By Annie Dillard.

The End of Nature. By Bill McKibben.

American Earth: Environmental Writing since Thoreau.
    Edited by Bill McKibben.

Banzeiro Òkòtó: The Amazon as the Center of the World.
    By Eliane Brum.

We Loved It All. By Lydia Millet.

The Blue River, a Tributary

Life Sentences: Literary Judgments and Accounts. By
    William H. Gass.

Lectures on Literature. By Vladimir Nabokov.

One Hundred Years of Solitude. By Gabriel García
    Márquez.

Stone. By Andy Goldsworthy.

The Tale of Genji. By Lady Murasaki. Translated by
    Arthur Waley.

The Woman in the Dunes. By Kobo Abé.

The Tain, from the Irish epic, *Táin Bó Cúailng.*
    Translated by Thomas Kinsella.

Molloy, *Murphy*, and *Watt*. By Samuel Beckett.

The Franchiser. By Stanley Elkin.

Doctor Faustus. By Thomas Mann. Translated by H. T. Lowe-Porter.

The Recognitions. By William Gaddis.

The Chicago River, Changing Direction

Chicago: City on the Make. By Nelson Algren.

A Street in Bronzeville. By Gwendolyn Brooks.

A Raisin in the Sun. By Lorraine Hansberry.

The House on Mango Street; *A House of My Own: Stories from My Life*. By Sandra Cisneros.

Touch and Go; *Division Street*; *P.S.: Further Thoughts from a Lifetime of Listening*. By Studs Terkel.

Man and His Symbols; *Memories, Dreams, Reflections*. By Carl Jung.

The Hero with a Thousand Faces; *The Masks of God: Creative Mythology*. By Joseph Campbell.

Metamorphoses. By Ovid. Translated by Rolfe Humphries.

River Styx

An Intimation of Things Distant: The Collected Fiction of Nella Larsen.

Omensetter's Luck. By William H. Gass.

Under Milk Wood; Portrait of the Artist as a Young Dog. By Dylan Thomas.

Of Mice and Men. By John Steinbeck.

The Theatre of Revolt. By Robert Brustein.

The Complete Works of Jane Bowles.

The Collected Poems of Wallace Stevens.

Bleak House. By Charles Dickens.

Middlemarch. By George Eliot.

Housekeeping. By Marilynne Robinson.

The Bluest Eye; Sula. By Toni Morrison.

The Color Purple. By Alice Walker.

Let Us Now Praise Famous Men. By James Agee and Walker Evans.

The Habit of Being: Letters of Flannery O'Connor.

Johnny Panic and the Bible of Dreams. By Sylvia Plath.

Mrs. Dalloway; To the Lighthouse. By Virginia Woolf.

Notes

Never the Same River, Never the Same Book

"Just as the river where I step" *Heraclitus: Fragments*, translated by Brooks Haxton (Penguin, 2003), 51.

The Hudson River, the Source

"I believe that we are" Alberto Manguel, *A Reader on Reading* (Yale University Press, 2010), ix.

"When I was a child" Marilynne Robinson, *When I Was a Child I Read Books* (Farrar, Straus and Giroux, 2012), 77.

"I feel as though I read your books" *Writers on the Air: Conversations about Books*, Donna Seaman (Paul Dry Books, 2005), 182.

"I've always hoped that someone" Francine Prose, *What to Read and Why* (Harper/HarperCollins Publishers, 2018), 5.

"If an event is meant" Diane Ackerman, *A Natural History of the Senses* (Random House, 1990), 127.

"When I grow up I cannot" bell hooks, *Bone Black: Memories of Girlhood* (Henry Holt, 1996), 76–77.

"*Little Women* is *the* book" Anne Boyd Rioux, *Meg, Jo, Beth, Amy: The Story of Little Women and Why It Still Matters* (W. W. Norton & Co., 2018), 120–121.

"Waste is a religious thing" Don DeLillo, *Underworld* (Scribner, 1997), 88.

"I've purchased and knocked down more liquor stores" Mary Dempsey. Article by Tina Trenkner (governing.com https://www.governing.com/poy/ mary-dempsey.html, 2006)

"Branch Library" Edward Hirsch, *Special Orders* (Alfred A. Knopf, 2008), 5.

"But the one outstanding fact" Bette Howland, "Public Facilities," *Calm Sea and Prosperous Voyage* (A Public Space Books, 2019), 99.

"I think fiction may be" Marilynne Robinson, "Imagination and Community," *When I Was a Child I Read Books* (Farrar, Straus and Giroux, 2012), 26.

"Billy took a Pez dispenser" Jay Cantor, *Great Neck* (Alfred A. Knopf, 2003), 31.

Reading High

"But words empower us" Terry Tempest Williams, *An Unspoken Hunger: Stories from the Field* (Pantheon, 1994), 57.

"To enhance the image" Anne Frank, *The Diary of a Young Girl: The Definitive Edition*, edited by Otto Frank and Mirjam Pressler, translated by Susan Masotty (Doubleday, 1995), 7.

"Heads up. Eyes front" Dorothy Sterling, *Mary Jane* (Scholastic, 1959; 1971), 42.

"I did not hear the word" Dorothy Sterling, *Close to My Heart: An Autobiography* (Quantuck Lane Press, 2005), 7.

"the landscape of nature writing" *Nature Writing: The Tradition in English*, edited by Robert Finch and John Elder (W. W. Norton & Co., 2002), 19.

"subsumes and moves beyond" *American Earth: Environmental Writing since Thoreau*, edited by Bill McKibben (Library of America, 2008), xxii.

"Its gentle christening aside" Eliane Brum, *Banzeiro Òkòtó: The Amazon as the Center of the World*, translated by Diane Grosklaus Whitty (Graywolf, 2023), 145.

"a scientific article about butterflies" Brum, 361.

"Storytelling will never" Lydia Millet, *We Loved It All* (W. W. Norton & Co., 2024), 222.

"We must alter what" Brum, 332.

The Blue River, a Tributary

"What works of art" William H. Gass, *Life Sentences: Literary Judgments and Accounts* (Alfred A. Knopf, 2012), 6.

"the good reader" Vladimir Nabokov, *Lectures on Literature*, edited by Fredson Bowers (A Harvest Book/Harcourt, Inc., 1980), 3.

"A stone is one" Andy Goldsworthy, *Stone* (Harry N. Abrams Inc., 1994), 6.

"It struck me" *The Tain*, from the Irish epic *Táin Bó Cúailng*, translated by Thomas Kinsella (Oxford University Press, 1970), 52, 53, 54, 55.

The Chicago River, Changing Direction

"To the east were" Nelson Algren, *Chicago: City on the Make* (Doubleday & Co., Inc., 1951), 14, 15.

"And we'd have a basement" Sandra Cisneros, *The*

House on Mango Street (Alfred A. Knopf, 1994), 5.

"must not contain nastiness" https://www.lib.uchi-cago.edu/crerar/about-crerar-library/history/

"the glory nights" Studs Terkel, *Touch and Go* (The New Press, 2007), 56, 57.

"On the north side" Terkel, p. 58

"It was Studs who" Sandra Cisneros, *A House of My Own: Stories of My Life* (Alfred A. Knopf, 2015), 35–36.

"...we also find in the unconscious" C. G. Jung, *Memories, Dreams, Reflections*, recorded and edited by Aniela Jaffé, translated by Richard and Clara Winston, revised edition (Vintage Books, 1973), 401–402, 196, 199.

"He looked at" Samuel Taylor Coleridge, C. G. Jung, *Memories, Dreams, Reflections*, p. v.

"And cymbals clashed" *Ovid Metamorphoses*, translated by Rolfe Humphries (Indiana University Press, 1955), 94, 130, 133.

River Styx

"Passing" Nella Larsen, *An Intimation of Things Distant: The Collected Fiction of Nella Larsen* (Anchor Books, 1992), 174.

"the piano was the" Edward Rothstein, "Made in the U.S.A., Once Gloriously, Now Precariously" (*New York Times* May 28, 1995), htps://www.nytimes.com/1995/05/28/arts/made-in-the-usa-once-gloriously-now-precariously.html

"Every day from nine to five" Sylvia Plath, *Johnny Panic and the Bible of Dreams* (Harper Colophon Books, Harper & Row, 1980), 152–153.

"Such are the visions" Virginia Woolf, *Mrs. Dalloway* (Harcourt Brace Jovanovich, 1925, 1981), 57.

River without End

Heraclitus: Fragments, translated by Brooks Haxton (Penguin, 2003), 27.

Acknowledgments

There would be no Ode Books and no *River of Books* without Jeff Deutsch. I am deeply grateful for Jeff's vision, passion, inspiration, and keen editorial insights. I'm thankful for Noor Shawaf's incisive reading, crucial editorial suggestions, and gentle piloting of the book. It was a keen pleasure to work with Matthew Engelke and I thank him and everyone at Prickly Paradigm Press for their warmth and expertise. I appreciate June Sawyers and her skillful attention. I am thankful beyond words for Sheryl Johnston and her extraordinary wisdom, proficiency, and generosity.

Profound and abiding thanks to the American Library Association for providing me with a meaningful working life. I am profoundly fortunate to have such smart, talented, dedicated, and fun colleagues at *Booklist*, and I am very grateful for their camaraderie and support. I am endlessly appreciative of our talented and caring reviewers and our readers. How lucky I am to have bookloving friends, and I thank them for listening to me talk about my struggles and conundrums with this book, especially Randy Albers, Angela Bonavoglia, Mary Mills, Nancy and Jon Fjortoft, and Emily Cook. I'm grateful, too, for the inspired and inspiring students and faculty I've worked with at the Graduate Creative Writing Program at Northwestern University's School of Professional Studies. Thank you to the Chicago Public Library, the American Writers Museum, the Printers Row Lit Fest, the Chicago Literary Hall of Fame, the Chicago Humanities Festival, Women & Children First, The Book Cellar, and Seminary Co-op for including me in exciting book events. Chicago's literary community is spectacular.

I miss my parents every day. I think of my sister all the time. We created the Claudia Ann Seaman Awards for Young Writers in her honor, and I'm so thankful for everyone at *Polyphony Lit* for making the awards an integral part of this global magazine's unique approach to nurturing teen editors and writers.

The river of books flows through our precious home, and I'm profoundly and eternally grateful to David for voyaging with me.

About the Author

Donna Seaman is editor in chief and adult books editor for *Booklist*. A recipient of the Louis Shores Award for Excellence in Book Reviewing and the Studs Terkel Humanities Service Award, Seaman is a member of the Content Leadership Team for the American Writers Museum and an adjunct professor for Northwestern University's Graduate Creative Writing Program, School of Professional Studies. Her author interviews are collected in *Writers on the Air: Conversations about Books*, and she is the author of *Identity Unknown: Rediscovering Seven American Women Artists* and *River of Books: A Life in Reading*.